IMAGES
of America

Champlain Valley Fair

The Champlain Valley Exposition in Essex Junction, Vermont, is seen from the air in 1939 facing east over the oval racetrack and grandstand. Cutting through the upper right, Pearl Street is edged with a string of homes (now mostly replaced by stores and fast-food outlets). Behind that, railroad tracks lead to the Five Corners intersection and the Central Vermont Railway station. Before the interstate highway, carnivals and circuses arrived by train, unloaded, and paraded animals and equipment to the fairgrounds. Compare this to the scene on page 92, after the grandstand and racetrack were rebuilt in a new location in 1966. (Photograph by Harry R. Stevens.)

On the Cover: The World of Mirth traveling carnival draws a crowd to its canvas tents for the merry-go-round, other rides, games, sideshows, and food at the 1941 Champlain Valley Fair. (Photograph by James Detore, University of Vermont [UVM] Special Collections.)

IMAGES
of America

CHAMPLAIN VALLEY FAIR

Stephen Mease

ISBN 978-1-4671-0850-8

Published by Arcadia Publishing
Charleston, South Carolina

Printed in the United States of America

Library of Congress Control Number: 2022934113

For all general information, please contact Arcadia Publishing:
Telephone 843-853-2070
Fax 843-853-0044
E-mail sales@arcadiapublishing.com
For customer service and orders:
Toll-Free 1-888-313-2665

Visit us on the Internet at www.arcadiapublishing.com

This commemorative book marking the Champlain Valley Exposition's 100th year is dedicated to the thousands of employees, superintendents, volunteers, and board members over the years who have made the Champlain Valley Exposition and the Champlain Valley Fair a century-long success.

Contents

Acknowledgments

This collection of photographs and memories looking back 100 years relied on the support of Champlain Valley Exposition leadership past and present.

Thanks go to executive director Timothy Shea and marketing director Jeffrey Bartley, who challenged me to update the exposition's history display in 2021 and then agreed that the next step to celebrate the exposition's 100th anniversary would be this book.

Likewise, in 1996, the 75th anniversary committee, led by general manager David Grimm, board president Robert McEwing, and sales and marketing director George Rousseau, published a comprehensive commemorative history book that informed some of the content of this book. And thanks go to all those proud staff members who preserved important historical ephemera, photographs, newspaper articles, souvenirs, and scrapbooks.

I owe gratitude to editor Cheryl Dorschner for her patience, for asking the right questions, and for keeping track of the details. My thanks to local historian Robert Blanchard for bringing his perspective to this project and to Green Mountain Video cinematographer James Heltz for preserving interviews done for the 85th anniversary.

I also appreciate Chris Burns, interim director of University of Vermont's (UVM) Special Collections Library, for digital files from Burlington area news photographer James Detore; the Library of Congress, Prints & Photographs Division, Farm Security Administration for work by photographer Jack Delano; Winooski photographer and former UVM professor Dan Higgins for his mid-1970s fair images; the Essex Historical Society; and a host of photographers over the years whose work is preserved in the Champlain Valley Exposition archives and used in this book. Unless otherwise noted, photographs are courtesy of the Champlain Valley Exposition.

Introduction

Small agricultural fairs sprung up all over Vermont beginning in the mid-1800s. Whether around the peak of sheep population in 1840 or the peak of dairy farming in 1947, people celebrated farming with fairs statewide. Vermont boasts one of the longest-running fairs—Tunbridge World's Fair, since 1867. However, the number of annual agricultural fairs has dropped from about 25 in 1900 to 12 fairs and field days as of 2021.

Among them, only one became the largest in size with the highest yearly attendance: 130 acres and more than 120,000 attendees—the Champlain Valley Fair. What is more, the Champlain Valley Exposition—its 501(c)(3) not-for-profit umbrella organization—transformed into a year-round, multifaceted event host and the largest-scale destination for regional community gatherings.

The origins of today's Champlain Valley Fair in Essex Junction, Vermont, can be found four miles east, where the Essex Grange fairs began in 1914 with a one-day event complete with food, dancing, horse-pulling contests, half-mile horse racetrack, and all the activities peculiar to old-time fairs.

The annual Grange fair in Essex Center grew to two days in 1915 and gained popularity so quickly that exhibits spilled over into the town hall and church and to tents pitched on the green of this little crossroads village. By 1921, the success of the fair was too much for the meadows west of the town common. According to a 1956 *Burlington Free Press* article, an attendee recalled, "When it rained, you could get in the muck up to your knees." It was time for "a fairgrounds with ample and permanent buildings, a racetrack complete with a grandstand, firm ground, and adequate room for a great many visitors and their vehicles."

In January 1922, representatives from almost every town in the county met in Burlington to organize, finance, and choose a location for a larger Chittenden County fairground. The Champlain Valley Exposition was incorporated in May as a stockholder organization with 1,000 shares offered at $50 each to help finance the purchase of land and buildings.

After six potential locations were discussed at a public hearing, Floyd Barnes's 70-acre farm on Pearl Street in Essex Junction, just west of the town center, was chosen. Located on firm, dry, sandy soil along the Burlington-Essex Junction trolley line and a stone's throw from the Central Vermont Railway station, it was a well-connected site with room to expand.

As noted in that 1956 *Burlington Free Press* article, "buildings do not grow up overnight. Nor does a racetrack dig itself out of cultivated farmland," so the first fair called the Champlain Valley Exposition was still held September 12–15, 1922, at the old site in Essex Center.

In 1923, the first fair in Essex Junction "was largely a tent show," reported the *Burlington Free Press*. "The first race spectators sat in what was described as a somewhat speedily erected set of bleachers" to watch the popular trotters and pacers circle the newly graded oval track. Yet it drew crowds nearly four times larger than the year before. Some reports say nearly 57,000 attended, with a profit of $7,357.

For the 1924 fair, a new grandstand sported fresh yellow paint and huge, thick black letters proudly proclaiming "Champlain Valley Exposition." A panoramic photograph taken September 12, 1924, by Burlington photographer Louis McAllister shows the grandstand and bleachers bursting at the seams with 4,000-plus fairgoers. A McAllister photograph taken four years later features acres of neatly parked automobiles surrounding the grandstand—a testament to the fair's popularity.

Buoyed by the success of its early years, more buildings rose: racing and draft horse stables, horse and cattle barns and show rings, an exhibit hall for commercial displays, and eventually, electric lighting so the fair could stay open after dark.

Although attendance suffered during the Great Depression from 1929 to 1933, by 1937, just 15 years after incorporating, the exposition called itself "Vermont's Largest Agricultural Fair." That year, fairgoers enjoyed a Broadway-style revue, daredevil thrill show, fireworks, four days of horse racing with purses over $7,500, and the largest carnival to ever visit the state.

However, four years later, in July 1941, when a severe windstorm leveled the cattle barn, the fair was unable to build a new one until 1946. The fair closed in 1942 and 1943 during World War II. And in 1957, for an influx of needed funds, the exposition sold about 3.5 acres with 700 feet along Pearl Street to developer Tony Pomerleau, who built a shopping mall.

Longtime board member Giles Willey, whose family's original 100-acre farm is adjacent to the fairgrounds, said that in the 1930s, his father sold 16 acres along Vermont Route 2A to the exposition. In 1962, Giles Willey sold an additional 65 acres to the exposition for $1, according to 1985 *Burlington Free Press* reports. This brought the exposition's real estate footprint to its current 130 acres.

Over the years, buildings were added, expanded, moved, repurposed, and replaced. But nothing was as dramatic as the fire of unknown origin on Sunday, July 11, 1965, that leveled the 41-year-old wooden grandstand seven weeks before the fair. Witnesses said the fire was spotted at 11:45 a.m., the roof collapsed about five minutes later, and the entire structure toppled to the ground just after noon. While there were no injuries, 5,000 people had been in the stands the night before watching a rodeo. The 1965 fair opened as scheduled.

A year later, the 45th Champlain Valley Fair opened with a new 3,000-capacity, steel-framed grandstand costing about $250,000. This grandstand was located 275 feet farther north, and the track was adjusted about 120 feet northwest to avoid a rock ledge at the southeastern end of the track. Three horse barns were also moved.

The new configuration allowed for a larger portable stage, outdoor bleachers, and on-ground seating to be set up in front of the grandstand, to bring the total concert seating to 10,000 people.

Perhaps even more significant to the exposition's long-term financial health was the 40,000-square-foot, heated, multipurpose structure built in 2000 for Nordic Spirit Soccer Club's indoor training. Five years later, a similar 10,000-square-foot addition with a wide attached hallway, restrooms, and meeting rooms was constructed next door. Combined, the Robert E. Miller Expo Centre South and North were named in gratitude for their commercial developer, Robert "Bobby" Miller of REM Development in Williston. These new facilities made the Champlain Valley Exposition a year-round venue.

But real estate, administration, and structures are merely the backdrop for what makes people return every year. It is the sights, sounds, scents, and tastes of the fair that define the Champlain Valley Fair experience.

The heaviest pumpkin in the Green Mountain State; pristine fresh vegetables, fruits, and flowers; well-tended potted plants; preserves, honey, and maple gleaming in glass jars; quintessentially local art and crafts; well-bred cattle, horses, oxen, sheep, pigs, poultry, and rabbits; the latest shiny farming equipment and cultivation methods—that is how founders envisioned the Champlain Valley Fair.

They were right in thinking that pride in local agriculture would draw exhibitors into friendly competition for blue ribbons, cash prizes, and bragging rights. And the fair would lure visitors from near and far throughout New England for a heady dose of the country life, novelty entertainment, games of chance, thrilling rides, and sweet and the salty, well-oiled flavors of fast-food favorites. It is a formula whose ingredients have not changed much in over a century.

It is not a fair without a midway where mysterious sideshows, games of chance, and dizzying rides reside. Since 1927, the fair has hosted nine carnivals including the World of Mirth, Vermont's own King Reid Shows, Reithoffer Shows, and currently, Strates Shows Inc.

Older Essex Junction residents recall that 50-car carnival trains would pull into the station late at night before the fair, offload equipment and animals (including elephants), and parade down Pearl Street to the fairgrounds.

The girlie shows and curiosity sideshows seem like ancient history. The carnival games still test ring tossing and balloon-popping skills, feats of strength, and aim, as always. But every year, the thrill level cranks up toward faster, higher, more extreme rides.

Harness racing—a centerpiece event from day one—remained popular for more than 50 years through the 1970s. The first fair in Essex Junction offered $11,000 total purses to winners. The next year, that jumped to $20,400, the largest sum of any Vermont fair at the time.

"Fair racing used to be a family type of event—people knew the owners, the drivers, and the horses, and they would go to the races to see them," Robert Whitcomb Jr. of Essex Junction told the *Burlington Free Press* in 1980.

Auto racing shared the oval track at the fair from its 1923 start, when just four drivers competed with stripped-down passenger automobiles as mostly a sideshow amusement. The American Auto Association–sanctioned races brought midget and sprint big car races to the fair until 1955. Drivers such as Barney Oldfield, Joie Chitwood, and Ralph DePalma were famous in racing circles.

But as auto speeds increased and cars became heavier and larger in the second half of the fair's century, so did the danger to drivers and spectators on or near this flat dirt track just yards from the grandstand. A proposal in the 1980s to create a paved auto racing track never made it past the town leaders. The last open-wheel auto race crossed the finish line in 1981. Nowadays, action-packed motorsports feature monster trucks, demolition derbies, and figure-eight races in a controlled setting.

Grandstand concerts also reflect changing entertainment tastes over the century. Simple band performances, vaudeville acts, and flashy Broadway revues of the 1930s through 1950s gave way to big names from radio and television.

The 1960s brought stars of the *Lawrence Welk Show*, country music, and family-friendly acts such as Gene Autry, the Cowsills, and the New Christy Minstrels. Through the 1980s, Nashville favorites, big band orchestras, and acts like accordionist Myron Floren, comedian Minnie Pearl, the Irish Rovers, Kenny Rogers, Loretta Lynn, and Roy Clark took to the stage.

The improved facilities and taking risks on new popular acts brought better-known musicians to the fair and summer concerts. Some of the brightest stars to play Essex Junction include Christina Aguilera, Justin Bieber, Jonas Brothers, Bob Dylan, Elton John, Toby Keith, Cyndi Lauper, Bruno Mars, Willie Nelson, Brad Paisley, Paul Simon, Britney Spears, Taylor Swift, James Taylor, and Neil Young.

An underlying goal of the fair is to introduce new things—farm practices, new equipment, the latest appliances, or technology. The indoor and outdoor commercial and industrial exhibits promise the convenience of viewing the latest models of whatever side by side. Vendors love a ready-made crowd. Shoppers know deals can be made, whether it is on the newest appliances, hot tubs, cutlery and pots and pans, or gargantuan farm equipment.

Fair food is irresistible. That once-a-year traditional indulgence is often only available locally at the Champlain Valley Fair. Treats include simple hot buttered ears of fresh sweet corn from the Rotary Club booth, corn dogs from the 75-year fair vendor Piggy Bar, cartons of fries from Al's French Frys, onions and peppers piled on a Mr. Sausage sandwich, a milkshake from the Dairy Center, or anything sweet from the Maple Sugar House.

For the more daring, fried Oreos, bloomin' onions, or deep-fried tacos attract long lines of fair foodies. Veering away from the booths, fairgoers enjoy the more social cooking demonstrations with local chefs, craft beer competitions, and even a martini bar to complement the beer tent.

That scent of fried dough and burgers wafting across the midway, the whoop of a winner choosing a huge plush panda, the shriek from atop the Ring of Fire or Zipper, aerialists swinging high above the crowd, an eight-year-old leading her Holstein calf to their first blue ribbon—all this and more is why the Champlain Valley Exposition's signature Champlain Valley Fair has grown to become the largest annual event in Vermont—aptly described as the "Ten Best Days of Summer."

Clearly, part of the exposition's plan was to become more than that—an invaluable resource to its regional community at all times. In upgrading the grandstand in the 1960s, it welcomed a wide range of entertainment in three seasons. And the new millennium additions of the Expo North and Expo South buildings opened the gates for Champlain Valley Exposition to become Vermont's premier, year-round host for large events, hosting thousands of people.

The exposition is home to the Vermont Flower Show, Vermont Farm Show, 4-H events, Northeast Street Rod Nationals, sportsman shows, home and garden shows, national recreational vehicle conventions, flea markets, roller derbies, and crafts, quilts, and antiques events. Its indoor-outdoor facilities attract equine events, hot-air balloon festivals, snocross races, and country music festivals. It is the winter home of the Nordic Spirit Soccer Club and Far Post Soccer Club.

And it is the year-round home of the Vermont Agricultural Hall of Fame, which honors farmers, producers, and people dedicated to supporting Vermont's working landscape.

When not hosting events, the fairgrounds are open to the public for hiking and dog walking. Many local teenagers learn to drive a car on the fairgrounds' paved roads before they venture out into traffic.

It also hosts high school and college graduations, mega-church services, fundraising marches and relays, state and national political rallies, and July Fourth celebrations. It is the place for send-off ceremonies for Vermont National Guard members being deployed and for welcoming them home.

When the coronavirus pandemic reached Vermont in March 2020, it tested Chittenden County's ability to care for its residents quickly and safely. The Champlain Valley Exposition was there to help, making its considerable facilities available to meet the urgent needs of the community.

The exposition pivoted to become a drive-through COVID-19 testing site for the University of Vermont Medical Center. The Vermont National Guard assembled an emergency surge medical center in Expo North and Expo South. The grounds easily accommodated long lines of cars picking up free food boxes from the Farm to Family donation program. In early 2021, the exposition was one of Vermont's largest mass vaccination sites, with more than 80,000 doses administered.

When it looked like the high school classes of 2020 and 2021 would have to forgo graduation ceremonies, the exposition hosted outdoor, drive-in-style graduations.

The state's pandemic restrictions canceled the 2020 Champlain Valley Fair and other events, but a series of socially distanced summer outdoor concerts and Taste of the Fair weekends supported food vendors and answered that craving for fried dough.

Thankfully, the Champlain Valley Fair safely returned in 2021 with its full 10-day celebration of agriculture, commerce, entertainment, and family fun.

In 2022, the Champlain Valley Exposition celebrates its 100th anniversary with a history exhibit at the fair, special events, and the publication of this Arcadia Publishing Images of America book, *Champlain Valley Fair.*

One

The Exposition Comes to Town

This red-and-yellow paper banner was made to promote the 1926 Champlain Valley Exposition. It now hangs in the exposition's administrative offices.

The open grandstand and bleachers bristle with 4,000 spectators for the harness races in 1924. Burlington photographer Louis McAllister's trademark was his panoramic camera, with which

Automobiles galore line the wide parking field at the 1928 fair. Visitors are here to see local dealers' new models under the long tent—said to be the second-biggest auto show in New England after

he photographed groups ranging from graduating classes to state police and summer camps. (Photograph by Louis McAllister.)

one in Boston. (Photograph by Louis McAllister.)

Announcement

The Champlain Valley Exposition announces its third annual exhibition, to be held at Champlain Park in Essex Junction September 9-10-11-12 and 13.

Though it was hurriedly put together we make no apology for our 1923 Exposition. Those of you who were here know it was worth your patronage, that we made no false promises and gave you one of the best exhibitions ever held in Northern New England. It met with instant favor. We propose to make progress every year and to make our annual show of value to exhibitors and patrons. How fast we progress will depend upon the support we receive. Out of an earnest desire to further improve the acquaintanceship and thereby foster the friendship of the people of Vermont and our sister states, the Management bids you one and all a most cordial welcome to our 1924 Exposition.

The development of all the interests that are allied to the farm, the home and the country estate is the object for which this Exposition was organized. The Directors have no other object in view. Not as a source of gain but as a means of uplifting and promoting agriculture, is their hope for the future of this Exposition. Conceived as an institution for the intellectual betterment of the citizens of this community, founded on the soil and its products, and conducted in a manner befitting the greatness and dignity of our State, we hope to progress by rapid growth and expansion to a foremost position among the fairs of New England.

May you find our program and exhibitions genuinely instructive, as well as entertaining. May your presence here and the impressions you gain result in bringing our people in closer relationship and may our annual Exposition become the time and place

"WHERE CITY AND COUNTRY MEET"

3

The 1924 premium book for exhibitors and fairgoers included a message that made no apologies for its first year at the new Essex Junction location and promised to continue to work to create a program and exhibitions genuinely instructive and entertaining. It expressed the hope that "our annual Exposition become the time and place where city and country meet."

INCORPORATED UNDER THE LAWS OF

VERMONT

No

Shares ONE

Champlain Valley Exposition, Inc.

CAPITAL STOCK $100,000.

This Certifies that ______________ is the owner of ONE Shares of the Capital Stock of **Champlain Valley Exposition, Inc.** transferable only on the books of the Corporation by the holder hereof in person or by Attorney upon surrender of this Certificate properly endorsed.

In Witness Whereof, the said Corporation has caused this Certificate to be signed by its duly authorized officers and to be sealed with the Seal of the Corporation this ______ day of ______ A.D. ______

1922

President

Secretary

SHARES $50.00 EACH

The Champlain Valley Exposition was incorporated in May 1922 as a stockholder organization with an initial offering of 1,000 shares at $50 each to help finance the purchase of land and buildings.

This west-facing view shows horse barns and some of the tents adjacent to the racetrack along with a simple booth selling ice-cold drinks, including chocolate milkshakes and grape punch. Eventually, these horse barns were moved to the north side of the track.

Champlain Valley Exposition News

Sec. 435½ P. L. & R.
U. S. Postage Paid
Essex Junction, Vermont
Permit No. 7

Vermont's Most Interesting Exposition
AT ESSEX JUNCTION
Aug. 25, 26, 27, 28, 29, 30, 1930

Wonderful Showing of
Cattle, Horses, Sheep, Poultry,
Swine and Agricultural Products
All Exhibits Are Larger
Than Ever Before

Boys and Girls

An entire building is required to show the Club Work of the Boys and Girls. This will be an Exposition in itself. Then there will be demonstrations and judging contests by the boys and girls.

All New
Vaudeville Acts

None of them ever seen here before. Sensational thrills of acrobatic stunts, juggling acts of much amusement, and many feats of daring, afternoon and evening. Will Hill's Society Circus—a masterpiece of comedy and thrills.

Gorgeous Fireworks

Dazzling fireworks of gorgeous beauty every evening with special features, many of which are produced for the first time. Set pieces of splendor almost awe-inspiring in inception.

Thrilling Automobile Races Saturday, August 30

Boys' and Girls' Club Work

By far, the exhibits of club work by the boys and girls, will be the most comprehensive this year of any previous time. For months these young people have been preparing for their exhibits and the showing will be specially interesting. In all classes there will be larger exhibits.

The 4-H Club members and leaders are striving to show the public the real meaning of their 4-H Club Pledge, which is

I Pledge:
My Head
My Heart
My Health
My Hands
For my Club, my Community, my Country.

With such a pledge, it is no wonder that the boys and girls are entering the Exposition with an enthusiasm that is inspiring. For months and months these young people have been working on their exhibits and they are going to show them with a proud spirit. Under the direction of Clara E. Salls, County Club Agent, they are just going to show the people what wonderful things can be done. There will be hundreds of exhibits by the boys and girls including all garden products, potatoes, corn, home-canned products, clothing, household articles, handicrafts, forestry, cooking, maple sugar products, picture stories and illustrated record books.

The exhibits of calves, swine, sheep, poultry and eggs promise to be the greatest ever. Then there will be demonstrations and judging teams by the boys and girls. The stock exhibits by the members of the 4-H Clubs is expected to be a revelation even to those who have watched the work of the young people in this line.

Special Music
The Burlington Military Band of 40 Pieces

Musical programs and special numbers by the now famous Burlington Military Band under the direction of Joseph F. Lechnyr.

The Burlington Band of 40 pieces will furnish selections throughout the entire length of the fair—afternoon and evening—and the band needs no introduction to fair patrons since its performances of past years.

Some of the Features of the Champlain Valley Exposition

Advance Grandstand Seat Sale
Amusement for Everyone
Animals—Wild
Arts and Crafts Exhibit
Automobiles admitted free Evenings
Automobile Races
Automobile Show—100 Cars
Balloons Free for the Kiddies
Band Concerts
Bees and Honey
Boys' and Girls' Club Work
Boys' and Girls' Exhibit
Boys' and Girls' Judging Teams
Burlington Day
Butter Producing Competition
Car Parking on Grounds
Carnival Company — Wm. Glick Greater Shows
Cattle Exhibit
Children's Day
Culinary Exhibits
Dairy Products
Demonstration by Boys and Girls
Dining Tents
Dominion Day
Duck Pond
Egg Laying Contest
Farm Machinery Exhibit
Farm Truck Exhibit
Fireworks Every Night
Fish and Game Exhibit
Flower Show
Forestry Exhibit
Fruit Show
Gates open at 7 a.m.
Governor's Day
Happyland for the Kiddies
Home Arts Show
Home Demonstration Exhibit
Horse Jumping Contest
Horse Racing
Horticultural Show
Hospital Tent
Industrial Exhibits
Information Bureau
Junior Red Cross
Live Stock Parade
Lunch Counters
Manufacturers' Exhibits
Many Free Attractions
Maple Sugar Exhibit
Margaret's Elephants
Merchants' Exhibits
Morgan Horse Exhibit
Needle Work Exhibit
Night Shows
Not a Dull Minute
Pet Stock Show
Pig Show
Pony Rides
Post Office on Grounds
Poultry Show
Rabbit Exhibit Featured
Races for Local Horses
Rest Tent
Sheep Show
Shepard's Contest
Society Circus
Special Prizes for 4-H Clubs
State Exhibit
Telephone Office on Grounds
Trained Dogs
Trotting—5 Days
Vaudeville Acts
Vegetable Exhibit
Winooski Day

Admissions

General Admission — Days Tuesday, Wednesday Thursday and Friday	$ .25
General Admission—Days Monday and Saturday	.50
General Admission—Evenings	.35
Children between 6 and 12 years	.25
Monday and Saturday, children under 12 years	free
Automobiles, teams and motorcycles—Days	.50
Automobiles—Evenings	free
Reserved seats in Grandstand (end sections)	.50
Reserved seats in Grandstand (center sections)	.75
Bleachers	.25
Grandstand, General Admission—Evenings	.25
No seats reserved evenings.	
Boxes, Days only, 6, 8 and 10 seats, each seat $1.00	
Single chair in box	1.00
Season ticket, not transferable	3.50
Exhibitor's ticket, issued to all exhibitors whose entry fees amount to $3.50 or over	3.50

Single admission tickets good for one entrance only. No return checks given.

Exhibitors', helpers' and privilege tickets good for one admission daily, are not transferable and will be forfeited if presented by other than person to whom issued.

Season tickets good for three admissions daily.

Gates will be opened at 7 a.m. each day and closed at 6 p.m. for the day.

They will re-open for the evening at 6.05 and close at midnight.

William Glick Shows

A new Midway will be a feature this year in the William Glick Shows. The management is fortunate in getting such a high-grade attraction of interesting shows and rides to come to Vermont. Previous to coming here the William Glick Shows were at the Ottawa (Canada) Fair and from here they will go to the New York State Fair at Syracuse. Certainly a Midway attraction that is good enough for the Ottawa and New York State Fairs would prove attractive at the Champlain Valley Exposition. This is a clean show with many interesting features and lots of fun for the old and young. Without question it is the best Midway ever shown in this Exposition.

NEW EXHIBITS—NEW SHOWS

This flyer, a veritable guidebook, was inserted in local newspapers and mailed to households in Chittenden County and across Vermont ahead of the 1930 fair. Note the emphasis on boys' and girls' clubs' events in the 4-H building.

Two

AGRICULTURE

A young farmer in the 1940s keeps his prize bull under control with a nose ring on his way to the cattle barn. (Photograph by James Detore, UVM Special Collections.)

Bringing cows from farm to fair is no small feat. It takes many hands and a calm demeanor to situate skittish cattle in unfamiliar barns, then ready them to show. Now that the fair runs 10 days, most dairy cattle stay five days. Switchover day is Wednesday.

While standing in front of the grandstand, a group of women talk with a harness race driver. For many rural Vermonters, coming to Essex Junction was one of the big trips of the year and a chance to catch up with friends. (Photograph by Jack Delano, Library of Congress.)

4-H dairy competitions allow young farmers the opportunity for blue ribbons with the Holsteins or Jerseys they have raised from calves. The 4-H competitions continue to be an important educational opportunity for fairgoers.

For many years, a highlight of the fair for 4-H members was the cavalcade of animals in front of the grandstand. Participants who successfully led their calves, ponies, or sheep would receive a shiny 50¢ piece as they left the track and headed back to the barns.

One is never too young to begin working at the fair. Preschooler Emily Fisher from Pittsfield, New Hampshire, started in 2005 with her family from Topline Farm. According to Wanda Emerich, superintendent of cattle, Fisher is still active in showing cows. (Photograph by Stephen Mease.)

Glenn Rogers of St. Albans, a University of Vermont Extension specialist for 28 years and a fair agricultural ambassador, encourages fairgoers to try their hands at milking a cow.

Horse and oxen pulling competitions were a mainstay of early country fairs and continue today at Champlain Valley Fair. Despite the dwindling number of teams in Vermont, the horsepower contest has not lost its appeal.

Gail Billings of Randolph and her team of red Holstein oxen walk in the afternoon parade. Billings and her teams, with names like Calvin and Coolidge, have shown at the fair since the 1990s.

E.H. Perkins Construction Inc. of Stow, Massachusetts, takes its Belgian six-horse hitch around the ring for judges at the draft horse driving competition.

Equine competition during the fair ranges from traditional English- and Western-style riding, 4-H contests, and cart driving. In the early 2000s, the exposition hosted Everything Equine, a regional horse event that included a trade show, demonstrations, and an evening horse show inside Expo South.

Gymkhana—speed pattern racing and timed games for horseback riders—is one of the most exciting, fast-paced competitions to watch. Here, barrel racing tests the skills of both horse and rider. (Photograph by Stephen Mease.)

Horse barns and show rings are located on the northern side of the fairgrounds adjacent to the campground, where many vendors, competitors, and the public make themselves at home during the fairs and other summer events.

Poultry superintendent Walter Bell took over the job in 1987 from his father, Fred Bell, who led that department from 1964 to 1986. The Bell family, from Swanton, was known statewide for their birds and expertise. They regularly took home blue-ribbon rosettes from the Champlain Valley Fair and the Rutland State Fair. Walter Bell retired in 2005. (Photograph by Stephen Mease.)

The water slide for ducklings amuses the young birds, and their quacking and splashing brings laughter and crowds to the poultry house. Swine, including sows and their piglets, make the other half of the barn their 10-day home.

The bleat of lambs, the scent of lanolin and fresh hay, the feel of wool, the sight of a newly shorn flock of sheep—stepping into the 4-H sheep tent awakens the senses.

Sheep to shawl shearing, spinning, and weaving demonstrations are a bonus alongside 4-H competitions among dozens of categories of rams, ewes, and lambs bred for wool and meat.

Kid-friendly, small-scale animals make Old McDonald's Farm the one-stop barn to see eggs hatching, baby chicks, piglets, and miniature horses and goats. Patience the Cow is a full-size model of a Holstein that youngsters may try to milk. Toddlers and parents appreciate the corncrib play area. (Photograph by Stephen Mease.)

The 4-H and fairs have gone hand in hand since 1914. Area 4-H kids work throughout the summer getting their exhibits and animals ready to show at the fair. Once they arrive at the fairgrounds, it is also time to have some fun, so on this morning before the gates opened, these members of the Shelburne Explorers 4-H Club took their calves for a stroll to the midway. From left to right are Maya Grevatt, Georgia Dixon, and Mallory Hillman. (Photograph by Stephen Mease.)

Three

Flowers, Vegetables, Art, and Crafts

The Champlain Valley Fair coincides with the summer harvest, so the time is ripe to show off those perfect tomatoes, peppers, and zucchinis. Entries are due the day before the fair opens to allow time for judging. (Photograph by James Detore, UVM Special Collections.)

This "Class of 2007" photograph of the Champlain Valley Fair superintendents, board members, and staff marks the 85th anniversary of the exposition. The 2006 fair was recognized as the "Top Fair in America," and received the Sweepstakes Award from the International Association of Fairs and Expositions. (Photograph by Stephen Mease.)

In the early decades, the fruits, vegetables, and flowers exhibits were in a tent, sponsored by Claussen's Florist, Greenhouse and Perennial Farm of Colchester. Today, those displays, along with bonsai, Christmas trees, giant pumpkins, and sand sculptures, are all indoors in the Expo North Centre.

Rachel Harrington of Essex Junction, plants and flowers superintendent from 1964 to 1992, organizes flower entries by cultivar, category, and division. Each year, cut flowers are judged on Saturday and Wednesday, so fairgoers view fresh flowers no matter when they visit.

Eight-ounce Coca-Cola bottles may seem unlikely vases, but they keep stems upright in the tight quarters of the tiered shelves packed with homegrown cut flower entries. Entrants vie for gold, red, and blue ribbons; best in the division; judges' choice; and best in show rosettes.

Frances Culver of Essex served the fair as superintendent of fruits and vegetables for 15 years from 1969 through 1984.

Pam Lord (left) of Shelburne looks on as Lyn Jarvis, of South Hero, prepares to taste a cake entered for judging. Jarvis was the producer of *Across the Fence*, a daily, 15-minute television program coproduced by the University of Vermont Extension and WCAX-TV Channel 3. He produced the show from 1975 to 2002 and included countless segments featuring the fair.

Canning fruits and vegetables was far more popular in the 1930s and 1940s, as this 4-H display indicates. Canning and preserving blue-ribbon competitions continue today, but on a smaller scale. (Photograph by James Detore, UVM Special Collections.)

Ruth Page (left) of Burlington looks on as a judge tastes jams and jellies under the watchful eye of Tod Whitaker of Shelburne, who began as superintendent in 1992.

Larry Myott (far right) of Franklin served on the exposition's board from 1977 to 1988. Throughout Vermont, he was known as "Mr. Maple" for his knowledge and activism promoting the maple industry throughout New England.

This observation hive of honeybees is typical of agricultural education displays designed to show fairgoers where their food comes from.

Fruit and vegetable contest judge Charlie Nardozzi of Ferrisburgh observes the weigh-in of large pumpkins and squash. Growing giant vegetables to display at the fair remains a popular pastime for Vermonters.

The size of the giant pumpkins continues to grow over the decades as breeding and techniques improve. The current record, 1,280 pounds, was set in 2021 by frequent winner Kevin Companion of Huntington. Runners-up often include John and Kerry Young of Jericho, Terry Keim of Williston, and Wilbur Horton of Springfield. (Photograph by Stephen Mease.)

Superintendent Helen Lawrence of Jericho began working for the fair in 1952 by handling the art and fancy work department. Its exhibit space on the second floor of the grandstand held quilts, rugs, blankets, tablecloths, aprons, dresses, bedspreads, and hundreds of other handmade items for sale. (Photograph by James Detore, UVM Special Collections.)

With the 4-H poster contests, club members share information about 4-H and some of their favorite projects. Youth from Addison, Chittenden, Franklin, Grand Isle, and Lamoille Counties are welcome to exhibit. Champlain Valley Fair provides 4-H with free facilities, admission for members and leaders, and the chance to win cash prizes with their ribbons.

The Blue Ribbon Pavilion is filled with home crafts, handmade toys, quilts, folk art, jewelry, clothing, and woodenware—all of it for sale. The top category winners earn a place in the winners' circle display.

Retail sales of handmade quilts, crafts, holiday decorations, knitted items, and wooden toys at the Champlain Valley Fair make shoppers happy, earn artists and craftspeople at least enough to buy more supplies, and support a fully local economy.

From left to right, Marcelle Leahy, her husband US senator Patrick Leahy, and superintendent Janet Dufrane check out the Champlain Valley Fair's art exhibit. The annual competition of paintings, photographs, sculpture, and children's art is displayed floor to ceiling.

Robert Waldo Brunelle Jr. of Jericho is a frequent contributor to Champlain Valley Fair art exhibits. A painter, illustrator, and cartoonist, he was inspired by the National Street Rod Association's fall weekend at the exposition; this work earned him a blue ribbon in 2005. (Photograph by Stephen Mease.)

Four

Free Attractions

Champlain Valley Fair celebrated its silver jubilee in 1946. An advertising flyer headline noted "Fair Back in PreWar Dress, Better Than Ever." Fireworks lit the sky all six nights. American Auto Association–sanctioned auto races returned to the flat track. And the carnival boasted 21 shows and 22 major rides on the midway.

Fort Ethan Allen Mounted Troops To Drill Wednesday and Thursday

Exposition Herald

Sec. 435½ P. L. & R. U. S. Postage Paid Essex Junction, Vt. Permit No. 7.

See Sensational Townsend Drive His Motorcycle Through a Board Fence

EXPOSITION CHALLENGES ENTERTAINMENT RECORDS

The 1933 Champlain Valley Exposition challenges all previous Vermont records for varied thrilling outdoor entertainment.

The challenge rests primarily on the number and quality of entirely new features instituted for fairgoers this year at Essex Junction, and is backed also by all of the popular features of previous years.

Here are some of the outstanding program numbers absolutely new this year, some of them never before presented in Vermont:

1. Sensational Townsend twice daily crashing through a board fence on a motorcycle driven at 60 miles an hour!

2. One-armed, one-legged Captain Smiles O'Timmons twice daily leaping 110 feet through the air into a shallow tank of water, each evening wrapping himself in flames as he starts his plunge.

3. Roman riding, other fancy riding, military maneuvers and artillery drills in front of the grand stand Wednesday and Thursday from 3 to 4 p. m. by soldiers from Fort Ethan Allen, accompanied by the Seventh Field Artillery band.

4. Van Sandt, 2:01, world record four-year-old trotter, one of 42 horses entered in the 2:18 stake trot.

5. Premiums for dairy cattle raised!

6. Baseball in front of the grandstand every afternoon at 1 o'clock with nine favorite Northern Vermont teams participating.

7. First Vermont exhibit of world's beautiful tropical fish, 25 [illegible] fish found in Vermont waters, and a score of other features.

Where before was there ever such an abundance of thrilling entertainment for all tastes? The Exposition issues the challenge.

PRIZE TO BIGGEST FAMILY AT FAIR

Thursday, August 31, is Family Day at the Champlain Valley Exposition—a new feature this year.

To the largest family of parents and children registering at the manager's office on that day will be given at 1 p. m. tickets on tickets admitting them to the fairgrounds, and reserved seat tickets to the trotting races in the afternoon and the fireworks in the evening.

So this family will have an entire day and evening at the Exposition absolutely free of charge, including grandstand seats to the special features.

Grandparents, aunts, uncles, cousins, nephews and nieces don't count in this contest. Just father, mother and their children. At least one parent must accompany the children. If both can come it's so [illegible]

Dives 110 Feet Girded In Flames

Fairgoers at the Champlain Valley Exposition August 28 to September 1, will see the most sensational vaudeville act ever witnessed in Northern Vermont.

Captain Smiles O'Timmons twice daily will plunge into space [illegible] daring, and breath-taking ability. It will feature the free vaudeville [illegible]

SOLDIERS TO DRILL

Roman riding and other fancy riding on the race track, military maneuvers and artillery drill inside the race track by soldiers from Fort Ethan Allen will be an added and distinctive feature of the program Wednesday and Thursday afternoons from 3 to 4 o'clock. The Seventh Field Artillery band will accompany these maneuvers.

For the first time in the history of the Champlain Valley Exposition the officers and men stationed at Fort Ethan Allen will be at the military reservation during fair week. In all previous years they have been ordered away on field maneuvers the last week of August and have thus been unable to take part in the Exposition, which is a near neighbor of Fort Ethan Allen.

The officers this year have greeted the opportunity of seeing the Exposition with enthusiasm and have offered the fullest cooperation in contributing a striking and popular program for the appreciation of the public.

Few people in the Champlain Valley and adjoining river valleys have had the opportunity of seeing Uncle Sam's regulars in action on horseback and maneuvering field artillery. Four units from Fort Ethan Allen will stage a special program of events far above the usual in military precision, rhythm and novelty. The Seventh Field Artillery band, which will accompany the riding and drill, is an outstanding group of trained musicians.

Wednesday, Burlington Day, and Thursday, Family Day, the [illegible]

In 1933, daredevil diver Captain Smiles O'Timmons, who only had one arm and one leg, leaped 110 feet into a shallow tank of water twice a day. In the evening, he would wrap himself in flames for the jump.

In the early 2000s, high divers wearing penguin suits billed themselves as the Penguin Arctic Blast show. For the finale, a "penguin," set on fire, dove into a 10-foot-deep water tank. (Photograph by Stephen Mease.)

In the 1930s, novelty balancing acts, acrobats, and high-wire performers—often formerly from traveling circuses like Ringling Bros. and Barnum & Bailey—took to the grandstand stage every afternoon. (Photograph by James Detore, UVM Special Collections.)

Page Eight — Champlain Valley Exposition, Essex Junction, Vt. — Aug. 28, 29, 30, 31, Sept. 1, 2, 1944

FIRST APPEARANCE IN VERMONT

Greatest of Thrill Shows

JACK KOCHMAN'S HOLLYWOOD

-HELL DRIVERS-

SEE The Spectacular DIVE BOMBER CRASH!

EDDIE STACEY, Human Battering Ram

TWO Thrill Days!

TUESDAY --- SATURDAY

August 29th — September 2nd

The greatest array of Daredevils ever assembled under one banner in front of a grandstand, including movie stunt men from Hollywood's film lots, former stars of the late "Lucky" Teter and Jimmie Lynch units, and a contingent of famous big-car racing stars in —

20 MOTOR CYCLE and AUTO CRASHES

THROUGH BRICK WALLS, PLATE GLASS and TUNNELS OF FIRE, CRASH ROLL-OVERS AND HELL-DRIVING THRILLS.

THIS AMAZING WAR-TIME THRILL SHOW

OPERATES WITHOUT THE USE OF GASOLINE OR RUBBER TIRES

A synthetic fuel pumped from a compressor into a specially-built carburetor powers the machines down the straightaway, while special cleated rims replace rubber tires.

DEATH-DEFYING DAREDEVILS BRINGING NEW THRILLS TO VERMONT FAIR-GOERS

BRING THE CHILDREN TO THE THRILL SHOWS

FREE ADMISSION (tax only) TUESDAY, AUGUST 29

25c (including tax) SATURDAY, SEPT. 1

For Children 12 and Under

DAY and NIGHT

Regular Adult Adm. Prices

ESSSX JUNCTION, VT.

Burlington Buses To Fair Grounds—4½ Miles

Crash-Drive Through Plate Glass

In 1944, Jack Kochman's Hollywood Hell Drivers made their first appearance at the Champlain Valley Fair. Note the disclaimer: the show did not use gasoline or rubber tires due to wartime rationing.

Daredevil motorcyclists rode more than 60 miles per hour around a six-foot perpendicular Thrill-O-Drome, presented by L. Harvey Cann in 1947. Between shows, the riders stood outside to drum up business. Motor thrill shows continue to be popular both in front of the grandstand and on the midway. (Photograph by James Detore, UVM Special Collections.)

Being a motorcycle thrill rider in the 1940s was an equal opportunity attraction, with at least three women highlighted on the Thrill-O-Drome's Motor Maniacs marquee. This may be Terry Strong, a movie stunt driver known in the show as the Blonde Cyclone. (Photograph by Jack Delano, Library of Congress.)

Page Four — CHAMPLAIN VALLEY EXPOSITION, ESSEX JUNCTION, VT. — AUG. 28

Fantasies of '44 -- Gorgeo

Spectacular Stage Shows

George A. Hamid, the Outdoor Impressario, will bring to the Champlain Valley Exposition every night during the week before Labor Day the glamorous bevy of young and charming damsels who will grace the huge stage in front of the grand-stand. This Revue of eighteen girls will delight the eye and ear with bewitching music and dance productions, a wealth of glittering costumes and colorful scenic effects.

Five big numbers are outstanding among this presentation of up-to-date and modern terpsichorean routines, featuring:

JITTERBUG NUMBER

In which are featured the winners of the 1944 Harvest Moon Dance Contest, held at Madison Square Garden, where notables of every branch of Show Business were in attendance and acted as Judges. This is a fast and furious exhibition of the modernistic dance that has taken the country by storm, with the famous FESTA TWINS holding the spotlight.

HAWAIIAN NUMBER

Dancing to the enchanting strains of Hawaiian music, the girls are presented in the authentic Hawaiian costumes in the swaying rhythm of the native dances of Hawaii. Again the FESTA TWINS captivate the audience with their Hawaiian gourdes.

MAG

A complete rev
audience this novelty
pate in rapid tap da
terialize all kinds of
public out of the ve
flowers and other ob
and mystifying magic

PICTU

The gowns worn
ever exhibited on an
the evening gowns b
shoe dancing rhythm
tional adagio team.

AM

This stirring pa
gorgeous show. The
costumes with militar
climaxing in the enti
tacle, in a tribute to

AFTERNOONS—EVENINGS

Tops In Vaudeville

...and Bill
WHITE BROTHERS — Comedy Acrobatics
MISS JEAN DAWN — Contortionist
THREE FRANKS — Aerialists
VICTORIA TROUPE — Stunt Cyclists
THE LEINARDOS — Society Dancers
STETSON BAND — George Ventre, Conductor

THE THREE FRANKS — Aerialists

12 -- Great Revue and Vaudevil

TUESDAY and FRIDAY — NIGHT and DAY — ADMISS
FREE TO CHILDREN 12 YEARS AND UNDER (

EVENING PRICES

(Gates Open For Admission Every Evening At 6:05 P. M.)

	Adm.	Tax	Total
Gen. Admission	.42	.08	.50
Grand-stand	.58	.12	.70
Automobiles			FREE

CHILDREN — 12 years and under Mon., Wed., Thur., Sat. Day or Night

Admission	.21	.04	.25
Grand-stand	.25	.05	.30

Tue. & Fri. FREE ... pay tax only

GEORGE VENTRE ENTERTAINS

WITH HIS STIRRING
STETSON RADIO BAND
a GEO. A. HAMID presentation

COMPLETE SHOWS—EVERY NIGHT TO MIDNIGHT

2, 1944

Page Five

Musical Revue

y Night

NUMBER

rst time presented to any
which all the girls partici-
same time appear to ma-
and before the eyes of the
es with birds, bouquets of
ng spectacle of fast motion
on of the producer.

E NUMBER

er are the most pretentious
ft pastel shade of colors of
ely with the graceful soft-
a charming and yet sensa-

ES ON

s a thrilling finale to this
d blue are featured in the
m number, baton whirling
g for a stage filling spec-
atue of Liberty.

ires -- 12

D STAND

R SHOWS

s Entertainment
and Colorful

DEVILLE

and THRILLS

ATTRACTIONS
AGED
E PLEASURE
LL AGES

COME EARLY—SEE IT ALL

VERMONT'S LARGEST FAIR GDOUNDS

Packed With

DAY and NIGHT ENTERTAINMENT

WORLD OF MIRTH SHOWS

GREATEST OF MIDWAYS

COMPLETE FAIR EXHIBITS

OPEN TO MIDNIGHT

VICTORIA TROUPE

T SHOWS — THE FAIR'S GRANDEST CLIMAX

George Hammond, the outdoor impresario, brought Fantasies of '44, featuring "a bevy of young and glamorous damsels who will grace the huge stage in front of the grandstand every evening." Many of the revue's big production numbers were patriotic. Also note, the fair's admission price was broken down by cost and tax. On special nights, children's admission was only the tax.

Puppies, kittens, rabbits, and other small animals for sale from local breeders tugged at heartstrings and did a brisk business. The practice was discontinued at the fair in 1991 due to growing concerns about the humane treatment of pets. (Photograph by Stephen Mease.)

Terrible Terriers of the Animal Circus wowed crowds in 1947. K-9s in Flight, the high-jumping Frisbee-catching rescue dogs, drew gasps in recent years. Animal acts will likely never go out of favor.

Lawrence Welk Show favorites—Larry Hooper, Bobby Burgess and Barbara Boylan, naughty boy Dennis the Menace, and Johnny Tillotson, a singer-songwriter who scored nine top-10 hits on the pop, country, and adult contemporary Billboard charts—all appeared at the 43rd Champlain Valley Fair.

Longtime Essex craftsman Fred Allen makes wooden pitchforks in a small tent in the fair's heritage trades area. While he whittles, he shares memories with onlookers. "I've been coming here back since the 1920s," Allen told a newspaper reporter in the 1980s. "It's a lot different from when they used to have the 'girlie' shows and all that drinking. A lot cleaner, too."

Children enjoyed elephant rides at the carnival in the 1940s. And a few days before the fairs, local people turned out at the Essex Junction station to see the arrival of the carnival train. After unloading, they would parade up Pearl Street to the fairgrounds. Since 2006, state law prevents elephants from performing in traveling shows in Vermont. (Photograph by Jack Delano, Library of Congress.)

Forty exotic and unusual domesticated animals strolled about the colorful big-top tent of the traveling children's zoo brought to the fair by Records and Burpee of Dudley, Massachusetts. Educational signage was often secondary to the chance to buy a handful of grain to feed the animals. Camel rides were an additional charge.

Sharks in mobile aquariums and trained bears, lions, and tigers starred in the most popular free shows for years. But as more people voiced concern about the humane treatment of wild animals, the acts were met with protests, and fewer such shows toured the fairs.

The Wild West Cowtown Rodeo brought bareback, Brahma bull, and saddle bronc riding to the New England town of Essex Junction in 1966. Rounding out this Saturday grandstand show were a Western band and rodeo clowns.

Superman distributes handshakes and autographed pictures to youngsters at Champlain Valley Fair yesterday. In real life, Superman is actor George Reaves.

'Superman' Likes His Job But Keeps Tongue in Cheek

By FRED ASHCRAFT

George Reaves, who began by singing and has reached the point of playing a kind of year-round Santa Claus role, is a man who takes his job with a professional twinkle.

For Reaves has virtually lost his own identity in that of a comic-strip man from the planet something-or-other by the name of Superman.

Two superheroes—Superman and Lassie—shared the stage in 1956. Actor George Reeves, who made the comic book hero come to life in the *Adventures of Superman*, and Lassie, the popular canine star of radio, movies, and television, both were part of the fair's Kiddie Kapers children's show.

Comic book heroes—especially those also well-known from television or movies—are regular visitors to the Champlain Valley Fair. Batman and Robin, from ABC-TV's series, visited in 1967. Spiderman and the Hulk appeared in the early 2000s. With very little crime to fight at the fairgrounds, most visiting heroes spend their time handing out autographs, posing for photographs, and riding in the afternoon parade.

De Yip Loo

Jerry Toman

APPEARING LIVE AND IN PERSON!

BATMAN

with ROBIN THE BOY WONDER!

BAM!

ZAP!

CHILDREN'S DAY

Tues., Aug. 26 11 AM & 2 PM

SIDE ACTS HELP MAKE SHOWS GO

Vaudeville acts that precede the main attractions have always been a strong part of the Fair's grandstand shows.

This year the Fair management has engaged some wonderful talent headed by De Yip Loo, the world's greatest Chinese magician.

Paul Lacross, the world's fastest, fanciest gunslinger, knife and tomahawk thrower will be back with his charming wife and daughter.

The Austins will bring one of the really fine balancing acts to the Fair stage and The Grimaldis will entertain with their musical poodles.

Most thrilling of the perforgers will be Col. Seabright, a sway-pole artist who performs hand stands 148 feet in the air.

Master of Ceremonies for the stage shows will be Jerry Toman, a master humorist and dialectician.

HELL DRIVERS

Mon., Aug. 25
2 & 8 PM

AUTO RACES

Sat., Aug. 30
1:30 PM

DEMOLITION DERBY

Sat., Aug. 30
8 PM

Hypnotist Steve Bayner is one of the most enduring free entertainment shows at the fair. With three shows every day of the fair, Bayner always draws an enthusiastic crowd to his stage on the Adsit Mall, and every show is different depending on the antics of his willing subjects. (Photograph by Stephen Mease.)

Local bands and musicians enjoy opportunities to play to the home crowd. Whether competing in a rising-star talent contest or playing dance music in the beer tent, there always seems to be music on the fairgrounds.

When giant sandcastles first became a fair attraction, they logically were located outside for the first few years. Local sand and gravel companies deliver, pile high, and compact the sand so that traveling sand artists can start their work a few days before the fair opens, then complete the sculpture well before the end of the fair.

In the ample space and high ceiling of Expo North Centre, each year's castle is now safe from unpredictable weather, well lit, and temperature controlled. Sandcastle artist Justin Gordon of Groveland, Massachusetts, has been creating giant works of art for more than 45 years. (Photograph by Stephen Mease.)

Randy Burns, the Mechanical Man, was a perennial favorite at the Champlain Valley Fair in the 1980s with his uncanny pantomime ability to impersonate a robot. He left many people wondering whether he really was a robot or a man.

Ah, the pig races—they return year after year with new porcine puns and even an ironic sponsor, McKenzie Country Sausage Racing Pigs. Fans do not have to pay for this pleasure, and the winning pigs get paid in Oreos. As an added attraction, some shows have a round of hot dogs—racing dachshunds wearing hot-dog bun costumes.

Oscar the Robot mingled with fair visitors daily for several years in the early 2000s. The blocky automaton (controlled via radio by an anonymous friend in the crowd) moved around the fairgrounds interacting with children and adults. Oscar would often wear a t-shirt emblazoned with his sponsor's logo. Behind him is the US Marine Corps Band. (Photograph by Stephen Mease.)

The Dixieland Strollers bring their music to all corners of the fairgrounds. Riding in the bed of an antique pick-up truck, they are also regulars in the daily parade. (Photograph by Stephen Mease.)

Five

CARNIVAL AND MIDWAY

The 1923 through 1926 fairs brought Brown & Dyer's carnival, whose reputation was well known from the Rutland and White River Junction fairs and many others in New England. The carnival boasted 16 shows, seven rides, and a funhouse.

In the early days of the traveling carnivals, posters called for local laborers to help set up and take down the carnival rides. Teenagers found it was a good way to earn enough cash to spend at the fair on rides and food.

Two young men add a fresh coat of paint to King Reid Shows' Ferris wheel seats before the ride was assembled for the 1963 fair. King Reid Shows was with the fair from 1957 through 1976.

Reid Lefevre, known as "King Reid," was a legislator from Manchester and was Vermont's equivalent of P.T. Barnum. He was a consummate showman, owner of the King Reid Shows carnival that traveled throughout the Northeast known for its side-by-side Ferris wheels.

The Round-Up uses centrifugal force for the high-spin ride that pins folks against the wall during the tilt.

It is hard to imagine the time and skill it takes to assemble the Mad Mouse roller coaster.

Carnivals at the Champlain Valley Fair offer dozens of different rides, designed to provide the exact amount of thrill that any patron might desire. For the more daring, there was the Roll-O-Plane, the Looper, the Spitfire, and the Silver Streak.

Flash Fire Destroys Tent Show At Fair; Menaces Entire Midway Officials Uncertain About Cause

Tent Empty at Time, But Two Girls in Show Receive Minor Burns As They Make Futile Attempt To Save Personal Possessions— Big Fair Crowd Praised for Its Behavior

Catastrophe might have put a premature end to the Champlain Valley exposition in Essex Junction late Saturday afternoon when a flash fire broke out in the tent occupied by the Gaieties Girls on the World of Mirth Midway.

With flames skyrocketing from the tent about 5, Saturday's huge crowd of fair-goers was prevented from becoming a panic-stricken multitude by calm, decisive directions broadcast over the amplifying system by fair officials. Speedy work by the Essex Junction and Burlington fire departments confined the flames to the Gaieties tent despite the strong wind.

Catastrophe was averted in 1945 on the midway after a tent occupied by the Gaieties Girls show caught fire on Saturday afternoon. The crowd was praised for following instructions delivered over the loudspeakers and not becoming "a panic-stricken multitude." Only minor injuries were reported.

Newspaper photographer James Detore of Burlington was in the right place to capture the dramatic fire on the midway in 1945, as carnival workers attempted to put out the fire before the Essex Junction Fire Department arrived on the scene. (Photograph by James Detore, UVM Special Collections.)

Performers with the Gaieties Girls show look on as their tent and all their belongings go up in flames in 1945. Two women received minor burns when they tried to retrieve their clothes and makeup. (Photograph by James Detore, UVM Special Collections.)

Firefighters and carnival workers survey the scene of the 1945 tent fire. Along with the tent, a wagon containing sound system and other equipment was also destroyed. (Photograph by James Detore, UVM Special Collections.)

Youngsters wearing multicolored beanies wait their turn to ride the merry-go-round. Beanies were popular in 1945 and among the prizes given at carnivals. (Photograph by James Detore, UVM Special Collections.)

Going to the fair in 1945 was a more formal event than the casual dress of today, although attitudes toward littering appear to have been more relaxed. (Photograph by Jack Delano, Library of Congress.)

The World of Mirth, with its carnival rides and attractions, came to Essex Junction in 1933 and 1937 through 1956. In 1947, it touted a complete facelift for the first time since 1941, thanks to an easing of material shortages after the war.

August 30, 31, Sept. 1, 2, 3, 4, 5, 6, 1948 Champlain Valley Exposition, Essex Jun

Enlarged "World of Mirth" Returns With 1,000 Tons of Fun-Making Equipment, 1,000 Laugh-Provoking Entertainers

Most Completely Equipped, Largest Outdoor Organization In the World; Everything From Mickey Mouse to Fattest Girl; Over 50 Featured Attractions

Every eye-appealing device known to modern decorative science has been incorporated into the physical structure of the World of Mirth, the largest traveling amusement company in the world, to enhance the attractiveness of its more than 50 streamlined features.

An ease-up in the shortage situation has enabled General Manager Frank Bergen to completely redecorate his midway and add many entertainment devices which are presented on tour for the first time. There are over 1,000 tons of fun-making equipment ready for the enjoyment of Fair patrons. Mr. Bergen has made every effort to add the finest equipment and attractions to the World of Mirth, protecting the show's reputation of being the most completely equipped and largest outdoor entertainment organization in the world.

The World of Mirth is especially designed to cater to the fancies of every member of the family. There is something that will catch the eye and spirit of all kids from six to sixty. There are musical revues, organized and rehearsed on Broadway, sideshow "freaks" gathered from all corners of the world, animals that do tricks and animals that must be kept caged and handled with utmost caution; Mickey Mouse is there — as is the fattest girl in all the world. There are cowboys and cowgirls, clowns and magicians, giants and midgets. And then, of course, the numerous riding devices!

There are 25 different rides. Each is designed to provide the exact amount of thrill that any patron might desire. For the more daring there is the Roll-O-Plane, the Looper, the Spitfire and the Silver Streak. Because a fellow must always take his "best girl" on a tour of the midway, the show still maintains that old favorite, "The Caterpillar," dressed in the gaiest raiment.

For the children there are the Merry-Go-Round and Ferris Wheels. For the smallest tots there is a streamlined train that is the very latest in the railroad design and three tiny carrousels that provide just enough of a thrill to satisfy both the child and the anxious parent. Fourteen ponies cater to the "cowboy and Indian" trade.

A free day at the fair was a reward for these teenagers with carrier routes for the *Burlington Free Press*. As a bonus, they had their photograph taken for the next day's newspaper.

4 CHAMPLAIN VALLEY FAIR, ESSEX JUNCTION, VT. AUG. 25, 26, 27, 28, 29, 30

King Reid Shows Midway Attraction Make Return Appearance At Fair

REID LEFEBRVE, stands before one of the mammoth cars that are used to transport the King Reid Shows from town to town.

Rides Galore at the Champlain Valley Fair. Giant ferris wheels, the fast moving caterpillar and lively octopus bid for the attention of pleasure seekers on the Midway.

Young Fry reign supreme in kiddieland where they have more than an acre of rides to choose from. A scene like this will greet youngsters on the Midway at the Champlain Valley Fair, August 25-30.

KING REID SHOWS
The WORLD'S CLEANEST MIDWAY

SIX BIG Days 6! Nights!

There's nothing like a ferris wheel ride to thrill the younger set—and some of the older set, too.

ADVANCE SALE
of RESERVED
GRANDSTAND
SEATS

Call or Write

P. F. JURGS Co.
150 Cherry Street
Burlington, Vt.
Phone UN 4-7491

or

Manager's Office
Fair Grounds
Essex Jct., Vt.
Phone TR 8-5545

9 A.M. till Noon
1 P.M. till 5 P.M.

Wild animal shows as well as rides and games are a big attraction on the Midway each year at the Fair.

A full page in the fair's newspaper promotion advertised King Reid Shows and its many attractions. The Vermont-based carnival company said that it had "The World's Cleanest Midway."

In the early days of the fair, Kiddieland rides were often just smaller versions of the big rides. Here, youngsters try their hand at driving, though a wooden rail keeps them on course.

Small gas-engine go-karts give kids control behind the wheel. Two iconic fads of the late 1950s and early 1960s date this photograph: the Bat Masterson t-shirt and the cinch-back khaki pants.

Illusionists, fire eaters, sword swallowers, and others take to the sideshow stage to entice fairgoers to pay for the chance to see them perform inside the tents. This group, called "Strange People," was with a traveling circus that played at the fairgrounds. (Photograph by Louis McAllister.)

As carnival sideshow attractions moved away from exhibiting people, midway barkers turned to attention-grabbing oddities of nature to draw a crowd. Many displayed normal creatures described in fantastical ways as "monsters."

Soak the Bloke is a classic attraction designed to separate fairgoers from their money by having a caged clown taunt passersby about their looks, ability to throw, and misses when they try to hit the small target arm that drops the "bloke" into a tank of water. The clown in this case looks about to be soaked, thanks to the good aim of the young pitcher. (Photograph by Stephen Mease.)

In the early 2000s, Reithoffer Shows' sideshow mix of oddities promised a fire-eating performer and an act with a boa constrictor. As many learned too late, the banner art outside was often better than the show inside. (Photograph by Stephen Mease.)

Winooski photographer and University of Vermont professor Dan Higgins (far left) set up a booth at the 1976 fair offering free postcard images. He spent the week chronicling fair patrons, carnival workers, and anyone willing to stop to be photographed. Higgins later turned the images into a gallery show and book. (Courtesy of Dan Higgins.)

Getting a family photograph taken at Scotty's Photos on the midway is a tradition for many people at the Champlain Valley Fair. Even in the era of phone selfies, many get a Scotty's portrait year after year. (Photograph by Stephen Mease.)

Carnival photographers commonly worked in tintype portraits because they were fast, inexpensive, and easy to make. A photographer could prepare, expose, develop, and varnish a tintype plate so that it was ready for customers in minutes. (Photograph by Jack Delano, Library of Congress.)

Fairgoers still find that dressing in vintage fashions and striking a classic pose is a fun way to bring home a memento of the day.

This west-facing view from the top of the big wheel at the Champlain Valley Fair takes in the midway, grandstand, agricultural exhibit buildings, and the sunset beyond. Many fairgoers time their

big wheel rides to the setting sun. The demolition derby can be seen in front of the grandstand. (Photograph by Stephen Mease.)

Strates Shows Inc. is the ninth regional and national carnival company to bring its rides, attractions, games, and food booths to the Essex Junction fairground's midway since 1923. (Photograph by Stephen Mease.)

Finally being tall enough to ride is one of life's great rites of passage at the Champlain Valley Fair. (Photograph by Stephen Mease.)

The Tornado is categorized as a "spectacular ride" by Reithoffer Shows—up two notches from "kiddie" and "thrill" rides. This one earns its legendary spot at the top of the midway due to its stomach-challenging spins and tilt-a-whirl action. (Photograph by Stephen Mease.)

Speed is a 120-foot-tall ride that tests the nerves of adrenalin junkies. Four passengers on each end of the arms sit back-to-back in seats that can swing 360 degrees while the arms rotate at up to 10 revolutions per minute. There is a 3.5 g-force acceleration on the riders. Even at $10 a ride, many found it worth the long lines to experience this Reithoffer Shows ride—at least once. (Photograph by Stephen Mease.)

"Quarter to Win, Quarter to Play" Fat Albert, one of the fair's most popular games of chance. While the colorful roulette wheel spins, a white rat known as Fat Albert heads into a colored hole, indicating the winner. A popular prize is a t-shirt that reads, "I'm Addicted to Fat Albert." (Photograph by Stephen Mease.)

Nothing beats the first taste of independence when hitting the midway on a warm summer Saturday night with best friends to check out the games, ride the Dutch Wheel, and eat cotton candy. (Photograph by Stephen Mease.)

Six

RACETRACK

In this off-season view of the original racetrack and grandstand, an access road hugs the contours of the track, and the small, two-story viewing stand used by timekeepers is across the track from the grandstand.

AUG. 30, 31, SEPT. 1, 2, 3, 4, 1937 CHAMPLAIN VALLEY EXPOSITION, Inc. 3

Track Records May Fall Before Fast Horses

Vermont Horses to Play Big Part in 4-Day Race Program

Entries From Stables of E. P. Cray of Bellows Falls, and Dunbar Bostwick of Shelburne To Compete In Very Fast Company This Year — Hambletonian Money Winner, Hollyrood Audrey, A Bostwick Horse, Expected to Meet Cray's Miss Vermont In 3-Year-Old Trot—Jane Azoff, 1:59½, Heads $1,000 Free-For-All Entries

Favored by a very fortunate "break", racing at the Champlain Valley Exposition this year is expected to surpass anything seen on the racing oval in recent years. Entries of fast horses have already been received in large numbers, according to a recent announcement by Frank Pine of Burlington, race secretary, and additional entries are being received regularly.

The entry of pari-mutual betting in Maine and Massachusetts racing circles has resulted in major operations on tracks of those states and the large purses have attracted a great many of the leading contenders on Eastern tracks. Many of the annual fair schedules will be seriously affected by this move, but the Exposition is fortunate in that its racing dates fall during a week of slack time on the major tracks.

No large meets are planned for Maine or Massachusetts during the week of August 30 to September 4, and the only meet which will conflict with the Exposition schedule is set for Kingston, Rhode Island. As a result of this break, many horses which would otherwise not have appeared, will be seen in action.

The track at the Exposition grounds has been under constant care for the past few weeks and will be in excellent shape for the coming meet. Known in racing circles as a good track, it will be lightning fast and at its best during the week of the fair.

Schedule 15 Events

Led by a number of Vermont horses, the fast steppers at the Exposition meet will compete in no less than fifteen events. The race program begins Tuesday, August 31, with the Two-Year-Old Trot, Three-Year-Old Trot, and North Country Special, Pace and Trot.

Wednesday's card lists the 2:20 Pace; 2:16 Trot; 2:23 Trot and 2:12 Pace. Thursday follows with the 2:20 Trot, 2:23 Pace; 2:12 Trot, and 2:16 Pace. The final day's racing, featuring the grand Free-For-All lists the 2:18 Trot; 2:18 Pace; Free-For-All Trot, and the $1,000 Free-For-All Pace.

Each of the races is run on the three heat plan, and racing fans will see nine heats on the first day of racing, followed by 12 heats on each of the following days.

Good Purses Draw Circuit Winners

The large purses offered for the Exposition meet have attracted a number of horses that have been consistent winners at Old Orchard and Agawam, hot spots of harness racing in Maine and Massachusetts. The $600 2:20 Pace on Wednesday has attracted such performers as Guy Putt, a recent Old Orchard winner in 2:04¼; Buck Hanover, Agawam winner in 2:05½; Anna Lee, winner at Old Orchard in 2:06, and Billy Direct, 2:02, an undefeated three-year-old pacer.

The $500 three-year-old Trot lists two very prominent Vermont horses. Hollyrood Audrey, owned and driven by Dunbar Bostwick of Shelburne, Vt., and Old Westbury, L. I., who recently won third money in the Hambletonian at Goshen, N. Y. Miss Vermont, well known to Vermont racing fans, comes from the racing stable of E. P. Cray of Bellows Falls, and recently won at Old Orchard in 2:05¾. Anna Lee, recently a winner at Old Orchard in 2:06, will be one of their chief contenders.

Free-For-All Climaxes Program

With an imposing list of entries, the $1,000 Free-For-All Pace is without doubt the best lineup on the card. Headed by Jane Azoff, 1:59½, some of the best on Eastern circuits are entered. Incomplete entries show:

Jane Azoff, 1:59½, owned by H. T. Fulton, Upper Steiack, Nova Scotia.

Harry G, recent winner in 2:04, owned by E. P. Cray, Bellows Falls.

Cash Counter, 2:05¼, owner, E. P. Cray, Bellows Falls.

John Judy, 2:01½, owner H. H. Buzzell, Belfast, Me.,

Earl West, 2:02¾, owner Paul Welp, Lewisburg, Pa.

Ray Henly, 2:01¾, owner Harry Short, Columbus, O.

Walter Dale, 2:00¾, owner F. D. Wilcox, Deposit, N. Y. Won all but one race in 12 starts last year.

Rip Hanover, 2:00¾, owner H. Toothaker, Somerville, Mass. Won four out of eight starts in 1936.

The Free-For-All Pace will be run Friday, along with three other races as previously reported.

Seating facilities for the race program are ample to take care of a large crowd, and prices are low. Choice grand-stand seats are reserved at 75 cents, with end sections going at 50 cents. Paddock seats in front of the grandstand are priced at 50 cents, and bleacher seats at 25 cents. In addition to the racing program each afternoon, there will be full vaudeville program as well as numbers from "Revelations of 1937", which will be presented between the heats of the races.

Shelburne Sportsman Enters Two Horses

Dunbar Bostwick Will Drive Hollyrood Audrey In Three-Year-Old Trot and Boyne In 2:16 Trot

Perhaps the horse with the widest national recognition at present of any of those entered at the Champlain Valley Exposition is Dunbar Bostwick's Hollyrood Audrey, which took third money in the Hambeltonian, peer of all American harness races at Goshen, N. Y., August 12. Going to the post a 30-1 shot, Hollyrood Audrey raced neck and neck with the country's best, finishing 6th in the first heat and 4th in the second heat to win some $2,500. The Bostwick horse faced the cream of the American harness racing crop in her initial appearance in the Hambeltonian. Hollyrood Audrey is entered in the 3-year-old trot.

Another entry from Bostwick's Shelburne farms will be Boyne, a winner on the Grand Circuit this year, a starter in the 2:16 Trot. Boyne won a recent race at Old Orchard, Maine, clipping the wire in the fast time of 2:04¼.

Dunbar Bostwick, of Shelburne, Vt., and Old Westbury, L. I., is an internationally known polo player. Only recently he became interested in harness racing, and is well on his way toward becoming a national name in the game. The July 14th issue of "The Harness Horse," speaking of Bostwick's racing at North Randall, Ohio, says:

"Dunbar W. Bostwick, of Shelburne, Vt., and Old Westbury, L. I., one of the recent recruits to our grand old sport, not only "done himself proud" this beautiful afternoon in winning the second division of The Ohio, but he and his dead-game trotting gelding, Boyne, were the chief thrill-providers in one of the most bitterly waged contests staged hereabouts in a long time. The unsexed grandson of the once famous champion, The Harvester 2:01, went a sparkling race, being second in the first and second heats, being beaten only a scant margin in each, but he showed no evidence of throwing up the sponge, neither did his young owner-driver, new to the game and pitting his ability against some of the most skilled professional reinsmen, appear the least discouraged, in fact seemed more energetic and determined, in the third heat, winning same in a spectacular and thrilling drive by the width of a "gnat's heel" then in the final, went to the top at the word, took matters easily and in the final drive, rushed Boyne the closing quarter in 29½ seconds, getting the verdict. Though this signalized Mr. Bostwick's first appearance in the Cleveland area, the hard-fought victory achieved by him and his ever trying gelding, earned him the admiration of the crowd and he was given a rousing cheer as he returned to the stand after he was awarded the decision."

Cray Lists Four Horses

E. P. Cray of Bellows Falls, well known for his stable of fast stepping horses, has entered three horses at the Exposition meet. Miss Vermont, starting in the 3-year-old trot, needs no introduction to Vermont harness racing fans. She has been a consistent winner, and has kept her record intact at the Old Orchard meets this summer. She recently won there in 2:05¾. Cash Counter, another Cray starter, is also well known. Cash Counter, 2:05¼ started in 12 races last year and won 10 of them. Cray's third horse entered thus far, Harry G. won at Old Orchard in 2:04¼, and starts in the Free-For-All as does Cash Counter.

RACE PROGRAM

Fort Ethan Allen Day—Tuesday, Aug. 31

2 year old Trot (closed)	$ 500.00
3 year old Trot (closed)	500.00
North Country Special—Trot and Pace	200.00

Burlington Day—Wednesday, Sept. 1

2:20 Pace (closed)	600.00
2:16 Trot (closed)	600.00
2:23 Trot (open)	300.00
2:12 Pace (open)	400.00

Governor's Day—Thursday, Sept. 2

2:20 Trot (closed)	600.00
2:23 Pace (open)	300.00
2:12 Trot (closed)	600.00
2:16 Pace (open)	400.00

Essex and Winooski Day—Friday, Sept. 3

2:18 Trot (open)	400.00
2:18 Pace (open)	400.00
Free For All Trot (open)	400.00
Free For All Pace (closed)	1,000.00

DUNBAR BOSTWICK

Harness racing was a key element of the Champlain Valley Fair from day one. It showcased some of the finest trotters in the Northeast. Large cash prizes for winners attracted the same well-known racers who competed regularly at Old Orchard Beach, Maine; Agawam Massachusetts; and Saratoga Springs, New York.

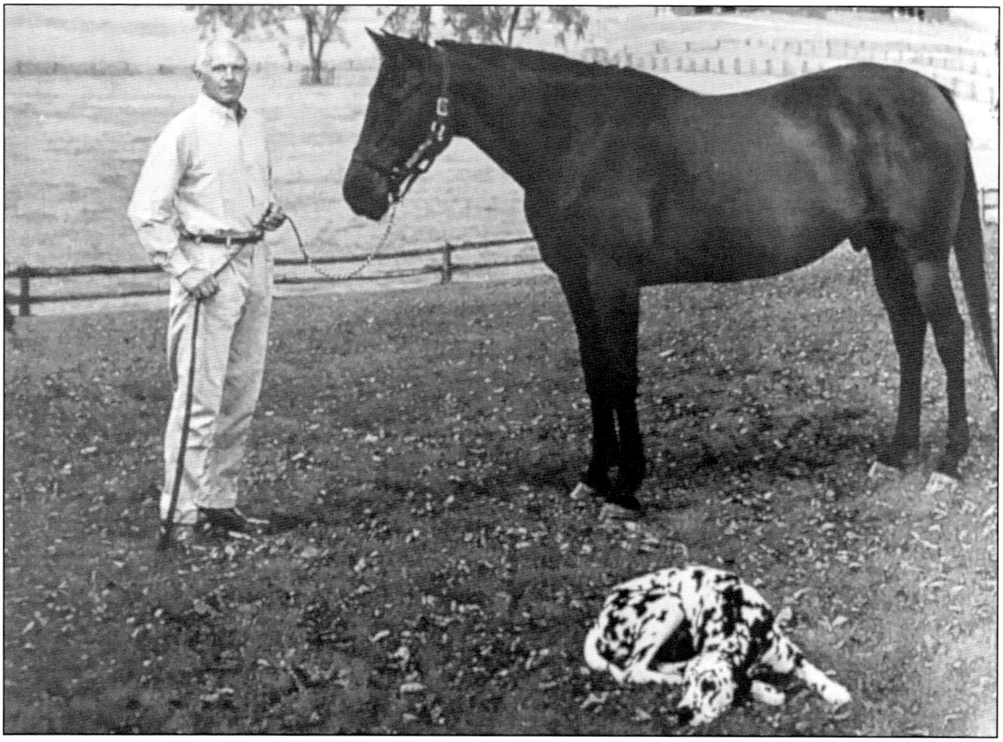

Dunbar Bostwick of Shelburne owned Chris Spenser, one of the greatest trotting geldings of the 1940s. The trotter won $205,250 during his career. Bostwick was also one of harness racing's most active supporters, treasurer and director of the US Trotting Association, and an exposition board member for 22 years.

A pair of harness racers head for the finish on the half-mile oval track. Race officials and special guests watch from the two-story viewing stand at the finish line. Spectators often parked in the center and enjoyed the races from there instead of the stands.

In harness racing, Standardbred horses (trotters or pacers) pull their drivers in two-wheeled carts called sulkies.

A harness race starts from behind a motorized starting gate. The horses commence pacing or trotting as they line up behind the hinged gate mounted on a moving automobile, which leads them to the starting line. At the line, the gate wings fold, and the vehicle accelerates away from the horses.

AUG. 28, 29, 30, 31, SEPT. 1, 2, 1939 — CHAMPLAIN VALLEY EXPOSITION, ESSEX JUNCTION, VT. — Page Seven

A BIG WEEK FOR SPORTSMEN!

15 Harness Race Events -- $8,550 Purses

4 HORSE RACING DAYS 4

TUESDAY — WEDNESDAY
THURSDAY — FRIDAY

RACES	PURSES
2:23 Pace (Open)	$ 300.00
2:23 Trot (open)	300.00
2:18 Pace (open)	300.00
2:18 Trot (open)	300.00
2:14 Pace (open)	300.00
2:14 Trot (open)	300.00
2 year old Trot (closed)	500.00
3 year old Trot (closed)	500.00
2:18 Pace (closed)	750.00
2:16 Trot (closed)	750.00
2:14 Pace (closed)	750.00
2:12 Trot (closed)	750.00
Junior Free-For-All Pace	750.00
Free-For-All Trot	750.00
Free-For-All Pace	1,250.00
	$8,550.00

CHAMPION PACER TO DEFEND LAURELS

EARL WEST — 2:01½ (HMT)

World's Champion pacer for three heats over a half-mile track. Record made at Champlain Valley Exposition, Essex Junction, Vt., September 3, 1937 in 2:01¾, 2:01½, 2:02¼ driven by Paul Whelp. Brown gelding foaled 1928 by Expay dam Illa Davis 2:24¼ by Tactician.

Will be back to defend his world record against a brilliant field of Free-For-All pacers.

Frank Pine, racing secretary, announced as this paper was going to press that an imposing list of race horses will be at the Fair this year.

Little Pat, winner of the Free-For-All Pace last year and undefeated this year, will challenge Earl West, who holds the track record of 2:01½ made in 1937. Miss Vermont, owned by E. P. Cray of Bellows Falls, won a feature trot at Old Orchard, Me., in 2:02¼, will go in the Free-For-All Trot. Another entry in that race is Kelly, driven by Pat O'Connell, both featured recently in Life Magazine's account of the Goshen meet. About 125 pacers and trotters will be on hand ready to race.

Promoting harness races was all about setting records and attracting the fastest horses to compete for top money. In 1939, the four days of midweek racing offered competitors $8,550 in prize money.

Ovila Richard of Winooski, shown here in 1944, was the timekeeper at harness races for many years. His own horses raced at the fair in the early 1930s. This photograph appears to have been taken while he was aboard a Lake Champlain ferry. (Photograph courtesy Helen Braddock.)

Kochman Hell Drivers Climax Thrill Show With Atomic Crisscross Leap

Death-Defying Stunt Performed in Open Cars

The most dangerous automobile stunt ever conceived will bring a thrilling close to the sensational program of Jack Kochman's World Champion Hell Drivers who appear at the Fair on Friday, August 29, beginning at 2:00 P. M.

It is the ramp to ramp, or automobile aerial criss-cross in mid-

turous ramps in the greatest ex hibition of precision driving and steering skill ever witnessed, as they twist and weave within in ches of each other while going a a mile a minute speed. Motor cycles riding the "Highway to Hades," motorcycles leaping through space and all the thrills known to stunting stars will b

The two-hour Jack Kochman's World Champion Hell Drivers shows include dozens of collisions, rollover contests, and precision driving over narrow ramps.

Thrill show enthusiasts love the dramatic rollovers and T-bone crashes that leave automobiles upside down on the track. The drivers often played to the crowd with a dash of drama. (Photograph by James Detore, UVM Special Collections.)

With a fanciful drawing of huge ramps and automobiles performing triple loops, this advertisement for the Fearless Greggs at the 1924 Champlain Valley Fair may have oversold the extent that automobiles would pass through the air.

It is a testament to the solid build of 1940s automobiles that whole families could sit and stand on top of them to watch the races at the fair. (Photograph by Jack Delano, Library of Congress.)

AUGUST 29 - SEPTEMBER 3 — CHAMPLAIN VALLEY FAIR, ESSEX JUNCTION, VERMONT

HARNESS RACERS come pounding past the grandstand in one of the thrilling heats at the Fair. Racing this year will be held on Wednesday and Thursday afternoons, Aug .31 and Sept. 1. Filly Stakes for 3-year-olds and 2-year-olds on Wednesday will each be worth an estimated $5,000 purse.

1960 Harness Race Program

WEDNESDAY — August 31, 1960

	Purse
Filly Stake — 3-year-olds (Essex No. 11) .... Est.	$5,000
Filly Stake — 2 year-olds (Shelburne No. 12) ....Est.	5,000
23 Class Trot	700
23 Class Pace	700

THURSDAY — September 1, 1960

	Purse
26 Class Trot	$ 500
26 Class Pace	500
20 Class Conditioned Trot	1,000
20 Class Conditioned Pace	1,000

DAN DANIELS, left, and BILL BROWN will be just two of the experienced United Racing Club drivers to take the track for the big car auto races on Saturday, Sept. 3. Time trials will start at 1 P.M., the first race about 2:30.

THE HELL DRIVERS, long-time favorites with Fair audiences, will be the thrilling attraction for grandstand audiences on Monday afternoon and evening, Aug. 29. Jack Kochman's daredevils will careen around the track in new 1960 cars, above, and risk life and limb in T-Bone crashes like that shown below.

BOB MARSHMAN displays his powerful midget racer, one of several to compete for the first time in Vermont on Friday afternoon, Sept. 2. Both the Midget Car Races on Friday and the Big Car Races on Saturday will be under the supervision of Sam Nunis.

Best Bread, Rolls to Win $50

Once again Vermont's good cooks will have a chance to compete for a prize of $50 and a diamond-studded gold ribbon pin.

This award will be made to the woman who bakes the yeast-raised bread, sweet bread or rolls judged "Best of Show." The prize is contributed by Standard Brands, Inc., makers of Fleishman's Yeast.

For additional information contact Mrs. Helen Lawrence of Jericho, Vt.

In 1960, the triple bill on the track was harness racing on Wednesday and Thursday, Hell Drivers Thrill Show on Monday, and the midget and big car races on Friday and Saturday.

There was very little space between spectators and sprint car racers, which was increasingly dangerous over the years as cars became bigger and faster.

It was always a challenge to keep the racetrack in shape, especially for the automobile races. The night before a race, maintenance workers spread tons of calcium chloride and thousands of gallons of water to keep the dust to a minimum.

A solid night of watching junk cars spin, squeal, and careen into each other with the goal of being the last car still moving in the arena is none other than the demolition derby. Survivors of early heats reconvene in the finale to determine who has the best driving skills and toughest car. (Photograph by Stephen Mease.)

While these winners of the demolition derby head home with a couple of hundred dollars in their pockets and impressive trophies for the mantle, their winning vehicles were usually headed directly to the salvage yard to be crushed.

In their heyday, big jet engine–style National Tractor Pulling Association events brought more than 3,000 enthusiasts to watch the contests. Classes of competitors include modified dragster tractors like this one, four-wheel-drive trucks, super farm tractors, and semitrucks. From 1978 until 2014, the Labor Day tractor pulls closed out the 10-day fair.

The National Tractor Pulling Association competitions bring many top Midwest competitors to New England for the Champlain Valley Fair's Labor Day shows. Vermont's most famous puller was Gardner Stone of Middlebury, who first started in Essex Junction with his mini-rod, single-engine model. He finished his career with a four-jet-engine dragster tractor with 12,000 horsepower.

US Freestyle Motocross Championship riders perform unbelievable stunts while 50 feet in the air on their bikes. The extreme tricks include this one called "Superman," where the rider lets go of the motorcycle and flies above it until it is time to land. (Photograph by Stephen Mease.)

The Joie Chitwood Thrill Show includes the dramatic trick of his speeding automobile appearing to be shot out of a cannon. Plenty of high-speed ramp jumps, reverse spins, and near misses round out his performances. Chitwood's racing career spanned from 1934 through 1950.

KSR Motorsports Night of Fire and Destruction in 2019 featured Doug "Danger" Senecal of Daytona, Florida, raising his arm in triumph after driving through a wall of flames. Senecal holds several records for long motorcycle jumps, and when not performing, he is a motivational speaker. He tallies 50 broken bones, a fractured skull, burns, and amnesia that lasted a year, according to his biography. (Photograph by Stephen Mease.)

Some high-flying thrill acts do not even need a motor, just plenty of pedal power to hit the ramps and take to the air. The show also includes a woman shot from a cannon and synchronized motocross aerial jumps. (Photograph by Stephen Mease.)

It took extreme measures to make sure there was enough snow in January 2006 and 2007 to hold the Rock Maple Extreme Snocross Snowmobile Races at the Champlain Valley Exposition. One year, snowmaking guns were used. The next year, truckloads of snow were brought in from vast parking lots at IBM. The one-third-mile circular course was complete with tabletops, hairpin turns, and extreme jumps. (Photograph by Stephen Mease.)

Monster truck shows include a half-dozen pickup trucks on steroids performing car-crushing jumps, donuts, and flips. (Photograph by Stephen Mease.)

Seven

GRANDSTAND

The grandstand, built in 1923, was the centerpiece of the fairgrounds with its yellow clapboard and huge black letters proudly proclaiming, "Champlain Valley Exposition." (Photograph by Jack Delano, Library of Congress.)

A fire of unknown origin leveled the 41-year-old wooden grandstand on July 11, 1965, only seven weeks before the fair. Witnesses said the fire was spotted at 11:45 a.m., the roof collapsed about five minutes later, and the entire structure toppled to the ground just after noon. This photograph of the fire was displayed in a history exhibit in the rebuilt grandstand.

Nothing was left of the grandstand when it burned in the summer of 1965. After the debris was cleared, temporary bleachers were brought in for the fair that year. Meanwhile, plans were in the works for its replacement.

Like long tentacle, shovel on heavy equipment reaches out to clutch and rip down remnant of concession stand at Essex Junction fairgrounds Monday. Grandstand and several concession stands were destroyed in Sunday fire.

Temporary Bleachers

Fair To Go On as Planned

The Champlain Valley Exposition in Essex Junction will be held as scheduled Aug. 30-Sept. 4, though the fair's 5,000-seat grandstand was destroyed by fire Sunday.

General Manager Harris K. (Had) Drury said Monday arrangements for temporary bleachers to replace the grandstand are being made. After Sunday's flash fire, Drury wasn't certain the fair could be held.

"We hope to have a new grandstand built for the fair in 1966," Drury added.

Several refreshment and concession stands near the grandstand also burned. "We're looking for ways now to accommodate our concessions and exhibitors," Drury said.

"So far as possible all regular programs and activities will go on as scheduled," Drury stated.

Meanwhile, cleanup operations began Monday. Some pieces of steel were all that could be salvaged from the charred rubble. Witnesses said the blaze started about 11:45 a.m. and in 15 minutes the 43-year-old wood structure had crumpled to the ground.

No one was injured in the blaze though at least one narrow escape was reported by a concessionaire cleaning up after the final performance of the Burlington Kiwanis Club rodeo held Saturday night.

Cause of the fire is unknown. Some reported seeing children playing around the grandstand Sunday morning and speculated the youngsters might have started the fire. Others thought it could have been faulty wiring.

There was another fire at the fairgrounds Monday afternoon, this one set by the cleanup crew after the unburned rubble and lumber from badly damaged concession stands were pushed into the hole where the grandstand stood.

While there were no injuries, it was noted in newspaper reports that 5,000 people had been in the stands the night before watching a rodeo, and results could have been far different if the fire broke out during an event.

The new grandstand was constructed with steel and concrete and finished in time for the 1966 fair. Costing $250,000, the new structure holds more than 3,500 people and contains additional space for dozens of exhibitors on the ground floor and mezzanine.

Fair manager Robert Adsit grooms the half-mile track at the new grandstand for the 45th Champlain Valley Fair. The 36-member King Family concert was the first grandstand show, featuring the popular King Sisters and Alvino Rey, a bandleader from the 1940s. Box seat tickets were $2.50; bleacher seats were $1.

The 1966 version of the grandstand reflects the style of the original, right down to the large block lettering on the back. Relocating the grandstand to the north made space for small stage shows, food vendors, and picnic tables on its south side. (Photo courtesy Sander H. Milens.)

Designers relocated the 1966 grandstand 275 feet north of the original location and adjusted the track about 120 feet northwest to avoid a rock ledge at the southeastern end of the track. Three horse barns were also moved.

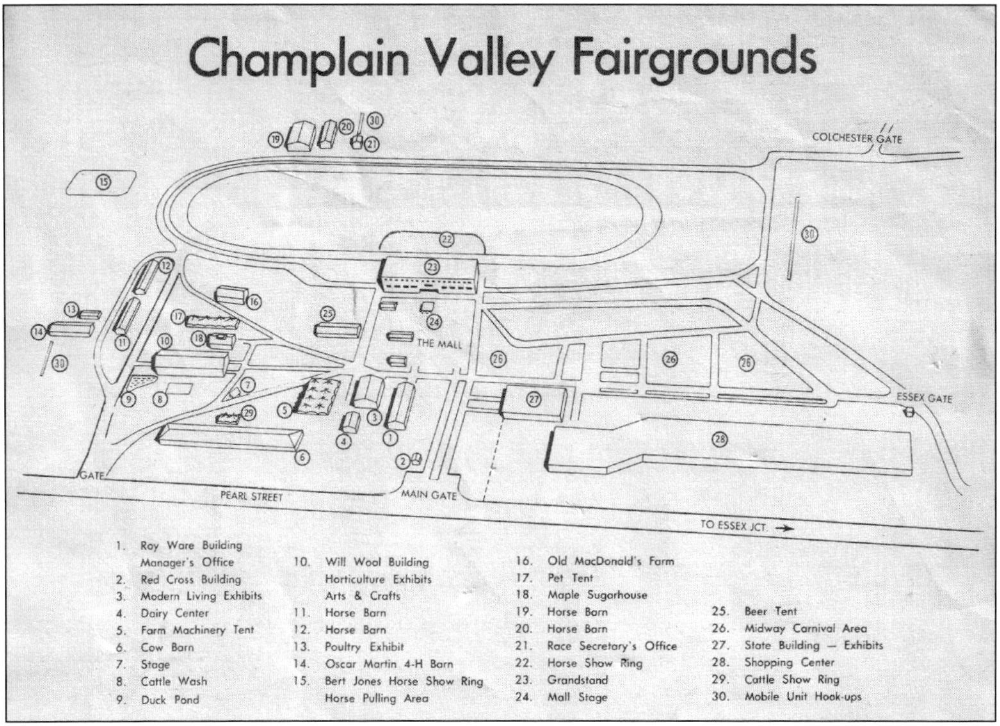

Champlain Valley Fairgrounds

COLCHESTER GATE
THE MALL
ESSEX GATE
GATE
PEARL STREET
MAIN GATE
TO ESSEX JCT. →

1. Roy Ware Building Manager's Office
2. Red Cross Building
3. Modern Living Exhibits
4. Dairy Center
5. Farm Machinery Tent
6. Cow Barn
7. Stage
8. Cattle Wash
9. Duck Pond
10. Will Wool Building Horticulture Exhibits Arts & Crafts
11. Horse Barn
12. Horse Barn
13. Poultry Exhibit
14. Oscar Martin 4-H Barn
15. Bert Jones Horse Show Ring Horse Pulling Area
16. Old MacDonald's Farm
17. Pet Tent
18. Maple Sugarhouse
19. Horse Barn
20. Horse Barn
21. Race Secretary's Office
22. Horse Show Ring
23. Grandstand
24. Mall Stage
25. Beer Tent
26. Midway Carnival Area
27. State Building – Exhibits
28. Shopping Center
29. Cattle Show Ring
30. Mobile Unit Hook-ups

This map of the Champlain Valley Exposition in 1978 indicates that the basic footprint is not much different today except for the addition of the Expo North and South buildings, entrance gates, and expanded parking.

The new configuration allows for a larger portable stage, outdoor bleachers, and on-ground seating to be set up in front of the grandstand, to bring the total concert seating to 10,000 people.

Eight

Big Concerts

Fans love to get close to the show to watch, cheer, and dance, thanks to the standing area. This 2018 concert with Old Dominion and Michael Ray demonstrates that there is ground-level seating beyond and more in the grandstand for those who prefer distance from the loudspeakers and protection from the weather. (Photograph by Stephen Mease.)

THE FAIR NEWS

GAMES SHOWS EXHIBITS RACES MUSIC DANCING

1960 - OUR 39th YEAR

ESSEX JUNCTION VERMONT

CARMEL QUINN, FONTANE SISTERS, HUCKLEBERRY HOUND TO HEADLINE BIG 1960 CHAMPLAIN VALLEY FAIR

Zippy The Chimp **Huckleberry Hound & Friends**

Children's Day at the Fair, Tuesday afternoon, Aug. 30, will be a happy bedlam when Huckleberry Hound, Yogi Bear and Zippy the Chimp prance on stage before the grandstand audience. Huck and Yogi are famous on television but newcomers to the fair circuit. Their personal appearance is worked out by the use of lifelike costumes.

Some years are better than others when it comes to headliners at the fair. In 1960, it came down to the singing trio Fontane Sisters, Irish songstress Carmel Quinn, Huckleberry Hound and Friends, and Zippy the Chimp.

Irish singer Carmel Quinn gained a national following after winning *Arthur Godfrey's Talent Scouts* radio contest in 1955. Her voice and performing style were compared to that of Judy Garland. She performed at both the 1960 and 1961 fairs. Quinn went on to perform on television and in Broadway shows, and her annual St. Patrick's Day concerts at Carnegie Hall sold out for more than two decades. (Photograph by James Detore, UVM Special Collections.)

Vermont's Biggest, Most Exciting Family Fair

THE BURLINGTON FREE PRESS
Saturday, Aug. 24, 1968

CHAMPLAIN VALLEY FAIR

AUG. 26-31

ESSEX JCT. VERMONT

Brenda Lee Stars at 47th Annual Fair

She's only 23 years old. But she's already a 15-year veteran in show business, standing now at the top of the entertainment world ladder, ranked as the world's number one female vocalist. This is Brenda Lee, petite dynamo, who will headline the stage shows at the 47th annual Champlain Valley Fair.

Brenda Lee started out on the *kiddie contest circuit, turned professional* at six *and signed her first* recording contract at eleven. She made her first network television appearance in 1956 and since has been a frequent home screen visitor via such vehicles as the Perry Como Show and shows hosted by Ed Sullivan, Danny Thomas, Steve Allen, Dick Clark, Bob Hope and many others.

Her recordings read like a hit parade who's who ranging from JAMBOLAYA, SWEET NOTHIN'S, I'M SORRY, TOO MANY RIVERS to FOOL NUMBER ONE and ALL ALONE AM I.

Her manager, Dub Allbritten, analyzed the Lee appeal in this way: "Brenda has always had three separate audiences. The kids liked her from the beginning, because she was one of them. Adults like her because she has the appeal of a little girl, with the aplomb of a woman; and ever since her records began hitting the charts, the teen-agers have gone for her. Since she appeals to all of those markets, she and her audiences can't outgrow each other."

Brenda Lee will be at the Fair for two evening shows on Wednesday, Aug. 28, and one night show Aug. 29.

New Channel 22 To Air Live TV from Fair

For the first time in its 47-year history, Vermont's biggest, most exciting family Fair will be covered by live television.

WVNY-TV, Channel 22, Burlington's newest television broadcaster, will station its mobile unit to cover events at the Fair commencing Monday and continuing until the Fair closes.

"We expect to telecast live for one hour each day from 4:30 to 5:30," says James R. Hodgins, director of operations, who is responsible for programming and scheduling at the station. "We'll be commenting on the action and interviewing winners and stage show celebrities. We're interested in bringing viewers in Vermont, northern New York and Montreal every event of high local interest, and the Fair will be the first of a string of such events covered by WVNY-TV."

Jack Siegel, general manager of the station continued, "We will have our mobile unit stationed between the grandstand and the main entrance. It will be outfitted with two cameras. Also we'll have a camera in the top row of the grandstand and another in the lower grandstand. However, we expect to be completely mobile and will be moving all around the grounds with our cameras."

The station's mobile unit was purchased in June from Sports Network Inc. It was most recently used to cover the PGA National Golf Tour. Inside the shiny white trailer are rows and rows of space age technical gadgetry including the two image orthicon field cameras for microwaving the local program back to the studio or transmitter site.

Local viewers will recognize the voices of Dean Slack and Tom Cheek, who will be interviewing and sports casting along with Mr. Siegel.

FUN TO SPARE...AT THE FAIR

BRENDA LEE, popular song stylist, headlines the grandstand shows with two performances Wednesday night and one show Thursday night.

CHANNEL 22 (WVNY-TV) — Mobile Unit, the first in this area, will be at the Fair to relay live daily telecasts to viewers in the Vermont-New York-Montreal areas.

Henson Cargill, Tammy Wynette Country & Western Favorites Signed

The Nashville Sound will echo through Vermont's Green Mountains Tuesday, Aug. 27, when two of the current top country and western recording stars, Tammy Wynette and Henson Cargill, arrive in Essex Junction to headline two evening grandstand shows at the Fair. Performances are at 7:30 and 9:15 P.M.

Tammy Wynette, billed as the "long-haired beauty from Alabama," joined the Golden Record Club with her recording of "Apartment No. 9." This was followed by a string of record hits including "I Don't Wanna Play House" and "Take Me To Your World." Today she owns the top-selling country and western record, "D-I-V-O-R-C-E."

In 1967 she joined talents with David Houston and their duet recordings of "Elusive Dreams" and "It's All Over" were two of the top records of that year.

Her voice, unusually pure and clear; her physical attractiveness and her on-stage polish mark Tammy as possessing that highly marketable quirk of nature called "star quality."

Appearing with Tammy Wynette will be seven young people featuring Don Chapel and Donna Kay.

HENSON CARGILL

"Skip-A-Rope" Brings Fame

The controversial record, "Skip A Rope," springboarded Henson Cargill to fame. Henson is a real-life

(Continued on Page 4)

Pop star Brenda Lee was 23 when she headlined three shows at the fair's 1968 concert series. She was the number-one female vocalist in the world, performing rockabilly, pop, and country music. During the 1960s, she had 47 US chart hits and is ranked fourth in that decade, surpassed only by Elvis Presley, the Beatles, and Ray Charles.

The stars of the *Lawrence Welk Show* hold the record for 15 grandstand concert appearances. The bandleader's troupe of popular performers, such as dancer Bobby Burgess, pianist Jo Ann Castle, and tap dancer Arthur Duncan, were favorites on the summer fair circuit. But the record for most Champlain Valley Fair shows—five—is held by accordionist Myron Floren, who performed most recently in 1988.

THE GOLDDIGGERS who will appear at the 1969 Champlain Valley Exposition as part of the grandstand show.

The Golddiggers, Las Vegas showgirl-style singers and dancers, performed at the fair in 1969. That year also brought country musician George Hamilton IV; the Cowsills, a wanna-be Beatles band of six brothers; and comedian and singer George Kirby.

AUGUST 31-SEPTEMBER 7, 1981 ESSEX JUNCTION, VERMONT

Here's Charley...and a stage Full of Stars

Charley Pride

Mickey Gilley

Johnny Lee

Rex Allen, Jr.

Margo Smith

Anacani

Bob Ralston

Bobby Burgess & Elaine Niverson

Charley Pride—Tuesday, Sept. 1
Charley Pride first hit the country music scene in 1965. Now, 38 albums and 43 singles later, Charley has gone from a country music giant to a popular stage and TV performer and international superstar. His awards, too numerous to list, include 18 Country Music Association nominations. Two shows at 7 and 9:15 p.m. Reserved seats: $6 and $4.

Mickey Gilley with Johnny Lee and The Urban Cowboy Band—Sunday, Sept. 6
With an impressive string of country hits to his credit ("Room Full of Roses", "Window Up Above") Mickey Gilley has brought a nationwide following to the Honky Tonk sound...and crowds to the club that bears his name in Pasadena, Texas. Sharing the grandstand with Gilley will be Johnny Lee who played in "Urban Cowboy" and recorded the hit single "Looking for Love" from the movie. Two shows at 7 and 9:15 p.m. Reserved seats: $6 and $4.

Rex Allen, Jr. and Margo Smith—Wednesday, Sept. 2
As the son of a famous singer, rodeo and movie star, Rex Allen, Jr., has not had an easy climb up the ladder of success. But a string of top ten records has recently been followed by the successful "Cup of Tea" recorded with pretty Margo Smith. While Allen ranges from Western to Nashville music, Margo goes from country to contemporary. In 1978 Billboard Magazine voted her number four Top Female Artist and her hit, "Don't Break the Heart That Loves You," was first on the charts for three weeks straight. Two shows at 7 and 9:15 p.m. Reserved seats: $6 and $4.

Anacani, Bob Ralston, Bobby & Elaine—Saturday, Sept. 5
Senior Citizen Day is also the day for three Lawrence Welk favorites. Anacani, nee Consuelo Gil Castillo, is the lovely Mexican-born featured singer with Welk. Bob Ralston delights millions of TV fans each week with his mastery of both the piano and organ. Bobby Burgess is making his third appearance at the Fair. This time, however, with a pretty new dancing partner, Elaine Niverson, who was picked over 32 other dancers auditioned by Bobby. One show at 8 p.m. Reserved seats: $5 and $3.

By the 60th annual fair in 1981, country music stars dominated the grandstand concert series. That trend continues, with the biggest headliners: Roy Clark, Alan Jackson, Toby Keith, Loretta Lynn, Reba McEntire, Tim McGraw, Willie Nelson, and Mel Tillis.

Country star Tim McGraw heads down to the stage barrier to greet fans at his sold-out September 4, 2005, concert. (Photograph by Stephen Mease.)

Singer-songwriter Taylor Swift plays the Champlain Valley Fair in 2007 with American Country Music's male vocalist of the year Brad Paisley, Jack Ingram, and Kellie Pickler. The Essex Junction show came at the end of the 35-city Bonfires and Amplifiers tour. Local country music radio station 98.9 WOKO sponsored the concert, and for many years held its own summer country music festivals at the fairgrounds. (Photograph by Stephen Mease.)

Darci Lynne is one of the youngest competitors to ever win *America's Got Talent*. With the help of her puppet Petunia, the young ventriloquist performs at the Champlain Valley Fair in 2019. Over the years, the grandstand series has included comedians like Larry the Cable Guy, Bill Cosby, Jeff Dunham, Gabriel Iglesias, Jim Gaffigan, and Garrison Keillor and his *A Prairie Home Companion*. (Photograph by Stephen Mease.)

Nine buses, nine semitrucks, and a crew of 90 people brought the elaborate 2006 Rascal Flatts Me and My Gang tour to Essex Junction for that year's biggest concert. The show was part of a 21-city tour by the Country Music Academy's group of the year that played before more than a million fans. (Photograph by Stephen Mease.)

Elton John plays to 10,000 Vermont fans on July 21, 2008. To celebrate the British rocker's 50th state concert, Ben and Jerry's created a limited edition Goodbye Yellow Brickle Road ice cream, which was chocolate with peanut butter cookie dough, butter brickle, and white chocolate chunks. All proceeds went to the Elton John AIDS Foundation. (Photograph by Stephen Mease.)

The Village People are among the many bands that play the fair concert circuit nationwide in order to rekindle relationships with their fans. Oldies bands and classic rock bands like Blue Oyster Cult, Joan Jett & the Blackhearts, and ZZ Top have also played at the Champlain Valley Fair. (Photograph by Stephen Mease.)

Nine

Exhibitors and Food

Squirting flowers, chattering teeth, and magic tricks were all stocked and traded at Lamere's Joke Shop in the fair's commercial booth section in 1945. Signs promise that shopkeepers will reveal the secrets of how to do the magic tricks after purchase. (Photograph by James Detore, UVM Special Collections.)

In case the latest appliances and deals on frozen food are not enough to attract a crowd, the C.P. Smith Supply Company employed Yodeling Audrey to bring customers to its booth in 1945. (Photograph by James Detore, UVM Special Collections.)

Handwoven rugs, crocheted items, leather belts, purses, and even shoes made by blind Vermonters were sold by the Vermont Department of Social Welfare Division for the Blind at the 1945 fair. (Photograph by James Detore, UVM Special Collections.)

Taxidermy grizzly bears, Alaskan sledding equipment, and a fur jacket displayed at the 1947 fair—part of Electra Webb's extensive collection—later became part of Shelburne Museum. (Photograph by James Detore, UVM Special Collections.)

The plastics industry came of age during World War II, so companies tried to sell plastic products to replace traditional materials. Here, seven Halliday Plastics representatives tout affordable new plastic aprons, tablecloths, dolls, and curtains at the 1945 exposition. (Photograph by James Detore, UVM Special Collections.)

The Champlain Valley's newest station, WVNY-TV Channel 22, brings its mobile broadcast unit to the fair for the first daily, live television broadcasts from the fairgrounds. The 1968 transmissions reached audiences in Vermont and as far as New York and Montreal.

Farm equipment manufacturers bring their biggest tractors and field equipment to display in the commercial building to entice farmers and wow the public.

When WDOT started in 1954 as a radio station, it set up a mobile trailer to broadcast its programming from the fairgrounds. Founder Val Carter teamed up with Fassett's Bakery, maker of Nu-Loaf and Sno-Flake Donuts, for a commercial that urged folks to "listen every day for on-the-spot broadcasts 1400 on the dial." (Photograph by James Detore, UVM Special Collections.)

Burlington Day Throngs At Fair Total 19,500

(Photos and other Fair stories, pages 3, 7, 9, 10, 11, 16)

A Burlington Day crowd of 19,500 attended the Champlain Valley Exposition in Essex Junction yesterday afternoon and last evening, fair officials reported last night.

Though this figure is 2,000 fewer than last year, officials called attendance "very satisfactory considering the weather." Total attendance for the first four days is up to 44,500.

Mayor J. Edward Moran spoke briefly. Stores and many business offices were closed for the afternoon in Burlington, Winooski and Essex Junction.

Harness racing began yesterday with vaudeville acts between races and the Fantasies Revue last night. These three features will continue today and tonight.

Also scheduled for today are the horse-pulling contests with more than 50 teams already entered.

Today is Governor's Day. Gov. and Mrs. Joseph B. Johnson will head a party of six that will include Neal J. Houston, executive secretary, and Mrs. Houston, Municipal Judge Edward J. Costello and Mrs. Costello.

A strategy in the early years of the fair was to declare a Burlington Day to encourage local businesses in Burlington, Winooski, and Essex Junction to close for the afternoon and boost attendance numbers by urging their employees and customers to visit the fair.

Steakhouse Road at the East-West Walkway intersection is a good place to start a fair food stroll to secure that once-a-year serving of fried dough, kielbasa with pepper and onions, fried tacos, or bacon-on-a-stick.

The lines to attend concerts often (conveniently) snake down Steakhouse Road long before the gates open, so it is easy to grab a bite from one of the tempting dozen food vendors along this main thoroughfare.

Fair Patrons Eat Ton and a Half Of Hot Dogs, Ton of Hamburg

Patrons of the Champlain Valley Fair were chomping enthusiastically away yesterday on their fourth mile of hot dogs after a splendid four-day exhibition of eating and drinking.

A check of concessions, followed by a hasty consultation with the slide rule, revealed that customers thus far had gnawed their way through a ton and a half of hot dogs, better than a ton of hamburgers and some 45,600 bottles of soda.

Reduced to bite-size, that's 33,200 hot dogs, or, if you laid them end-to-end, just short of three miles, or $8,300 worth of hot dogs.

The trusty medium of statistics reduces the hamburger poundage to 19,200 'burgers.

And the soft drink consumption figures out at 2,287 gallons.

Despite the totals, one concession operator held out for the good old days.

"You should have been here two years ago," he said. "That year, they really ate. Wasn't safe to put your hands on the counter to pick up change—somebody was liable to bite it off."

A clever newspaper reporter looking for a new angle on an old story did the math on how much food is consumed at the fair. While tough to fact-check, it is clear that hot dogs were the favorite that year by a mile, and in the vendors' eyes, business could always be better.

Maple coffee, maple frosted donuts, maple milkshakes, maple creemees, maple bread, maple cotton candy—it is maple all day and all night in the Maple Sugar House, operated by the Chittenden County Maple Sugarmakers Association. Blue-ribbon maple syrup is displayed along with an exhibit on sugarmaking.

The Piggy Bar, famous for its freshly made corn dogs, has been serving up this fair delicacy for 75 years.

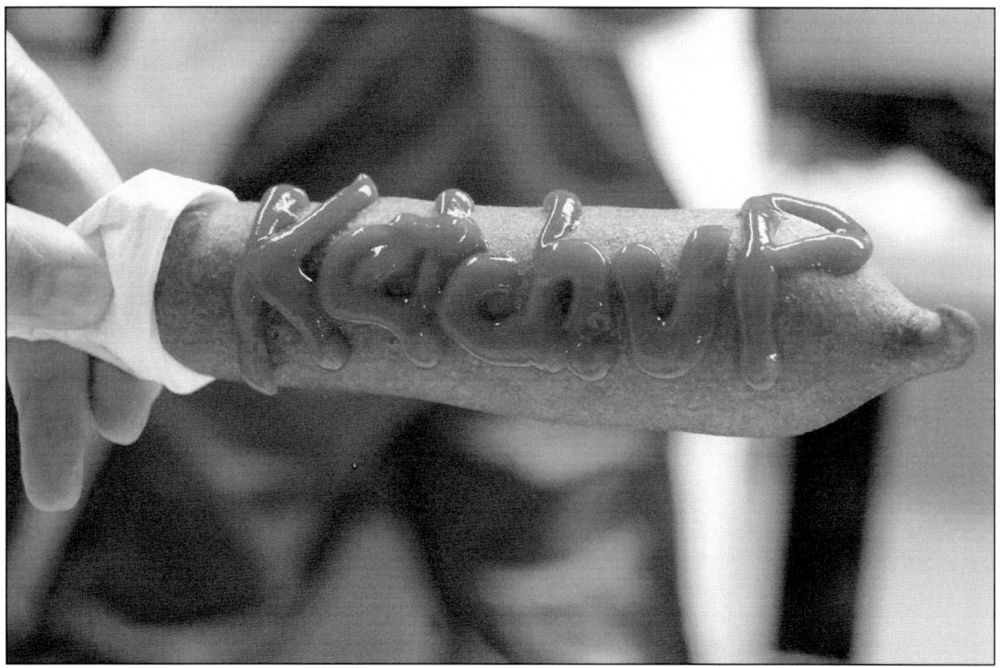

Ketchup with a corn dog while you catch up with friends at the Piggy Bar. If one is lucky, the vendor will spell it out. (Photograph by Stephen Mease.)

Many civic not-for-profits, such as the local Rotary International, serve corn on the cob, hamburgers, hot dogs, and more as part of their main annual fundraising efforts. (Photograph by Stephen Mease.)

Al and Genevieve Rusterholtz started Al's French Frys in South Burlington and opened their first booth at the fair in 1946. The business still serves homemade fast food and nostalgia. It was purchased by Bill and Lee Bissonette in 1983. Bill and his son Shane now own its flagship retro destination and operate Al's French Frys stands and the Oasis smoothie stand at the fairgrounds. (Photograph by Stephen Mease.)

Actor, author, and "blue-collar comedian" Rusty DeWees of Elmore promotes his well-known one-man show, *The Logger*, along with autographed merchandise. (Photograph by Stephen Mease.)

Fresh Vermont apples from South Hero are in every bite of Allenholm Farms' homemade apple pie. Make that à la mode. Ray Allen, the seventh generation to run the orchard, and his wife, Peg Allen, were icons of Vermont agriculture. Two younger generations of the family now operate Allenholm Farms.

Ten

Year-Round Community

The fairgrounds are a regional community gathering place. The Town of Essex was one of several Vermont towns that celebrated its bicentennial in 1963. It chose the nearby Champlain Valley Exposition for its big event.

Horatio "Ray" Jenkins of Essex Junction was maintenance coordinator at Champlain Valley Exposition for 28 years after he retired from IBM in 1971. In 2007, still employed at age 101, he was honored as America's oldest worker by Experience Works Prime Time Awards of Washington, DC. His son Robert Jenkins is director of facilities at the exposition, a job he has held since 2007. (Photograph by Stephen Mease.)

From left to right are friend of the fair and man behind the Robert E. Miller Expo Centre Robert "Bobby" Miller, his son Timothy Miller, 2007 board members Christina Inslee and Jane Clifford, and Reithoffer Shows owner Patrick Reithoffer. After a memorial service for Bobby Miller on February 12, 2020, executive director Timothy Shea said, "The exposition would not be what it is today without his vision and enthusiasm." (Photograph by Stephen Mease.)

Curly the Cow, the fair's mascot in the early 2000s, is surrounded by elementary-age readers who earned free admission to the fair and a new book because they participated in their local library's Read and Win program, sponsored by the Champlain Valley Exposition and IBM in Essex Junction. (Photograph by Stephen Mease.)

Exposition board president Matthew Stevens (right) contends with a playful Dalmatian on the Budweiser Clydesdale wagon before the fair's daily 5:00 p.m. parade through the fairgrounds. (Photograph by Stephen Mease.)

Harris "Had" Drury (left), fair manager from 1937 to 1973, and James Grow, treasurer from 1934 to 1940 and 1956 to 1966, talk in front of the grandstand during the 1939 fair. (Photograph by Jack Delano, Library of Congress.)

Robert Adsit Jr., general manager of the fair from 1977 to 1988 and board president and director from 1959 to 1989, is the namesake of Bob Adsit Mall, a green behind the grandstand.

From left to right, general manager David Grimm and Gov. James Douglas welcome British rocker Elton John to Vermont before his 50th state concert in July 2008. Elton John's first US show was in California in 1970, but he said it took him almost 40 years to perform in the last one—Vermont. (Photograph by Stephen Mease.)

Fair executive director Timothy Shea (left) and Gov. Phil Scott assist with the 2018 opening day 4-H ribbon-cutting ceremony. (Photograph by Stephen Mease.)

Sen. Patrick Leahy's visits to the fair include tours of agricultural exhibits and barns, art shows, and 4-H displays. Here, he poses with Champlain Valley Fair office support staff.

In 2006, then US representative Bernie Sanders; his wife, Jane Sanders; and their grandson Cole Ewoldsen enjoy an afternoon at the fair talking with friends and constituents. Sanders became one of Vermont's US senators in 2007 and ran for president in 2016 and 2020. (Photograph by Stephen Mease.)

In 1996, Vermont governor Howard Dean helped promote the pig races during Governor's Day at the 75th anniversary fair. He served as governor from 1991 until 2003 and ran for president in 2004.

US representative Peter Welch speaks at the annual Vermont Agricultural Hall of Fame luncheon during the Champlain Valley Fair. State dignitaries often attend to present the awards. (Photograph by Stephen Mease.)

The NBC *Today* show's beloved weatherman Willard Scott broadcast his national weather forecasts from the fair in 1992. One of his segments included trying a famous Mr. Sausage sandwich.

Ray Allen of South Hero, a longtime Champlain Valley Exposition board member and past president, wore many hats during the annual fair. Here, he monitors the fair's official weather station. The fair took out weather insurance on major concerts but never collected for a loss.

The new pedestrian gate and ticket booth were part of a Pearl Street revitalization project with the Village of Essex Junction in 2010 to improve sidewalks and lighting and to slow traffic on the busy street. The architecture is reminiscent of train or trolley stations. (Photograph by Stephen Mease.)

Not located on the front Pearl Street side of the fair, the main entrance that most people use is called "the red gate." It is the fair's "back door," adjacent to the parking lots and the Robert E. Miller Expo Centre. (Photograph by Stephen Mease.)

A partnership with Nordic Spirit Soccer Club in 1999 was the springboard to build the Robert E. Miller Expo Centre in 2000, and five years later, add the Expo North building for the Far Post Soccer Club and special events. These were necessary to meet the demand for indoor training and playing space for the area's youth soccer during winter. And this gave the exposition the ability to host large trade shows, music festivals, conferences, and special events year-round.

The National Street Rod Association's three-day gathering takes over the fairgrounds, bringing hundreds of street rods from around New England and beyond to Essex Junction. The annual mid-September event is welcomed by local hospitality and tourism businesses just ahead of the traditional Vermont fall foliage season.

For many years, the Essex Alliance Church held its traditional Easter weekend services at the Robert E. Miller Expo Centre to accommodate huge crowds drawn to its elaborate stage productions featuring bands and choral groups. (Photograph by Stephen Mease.)

The 130-acre Champlain Valley Exposition hosts several national recreational vehicle rallies, including the Family Motor Coach Association and the Wally Byam Caravan Club Airstream convention. In 2006, the BMW Motorcycle Owners Association held its annual International Rally in late July.

Circus Smirkus, a youth circus and summer camp based in Greensboro, starts its two-month New England road tour at the Champlain Valley Exposition. The freshly auditioned troupers, ages 10 to 18—backed by professional coaches, cooks, musicians, and crew—perform to sold-out crowds in a 750-seat European-style one-ring big top tent. (Photograph by Stephen Mease.)

Sen. Bernie Sanders, surrounded by his family, held large rallies at the exposition during both his runs for president. His March 2020 town meeting/primary day rally was the last large-scale event held at the exposition before the COVID-19 pandemic forced all events to be canceled. (Photograph by Stephen Mease.)

The Vermont Agricultural Hall of Fame also calls the exposition home. More than 90 Vermonters have been inducted since 2003. Awards luncheons for the inductees and their families are held during the Champlain Valley Fair.

In 2021, Agricultural Hall of Fame inductee Polly Whitcomb McEwing of Essex Junction (first row, center) was honored for 50 years of running the North Williston Cattle Company in Essex and Williston. She cofounded the Champlain Valley Fair Dairy Center in the 1960s, which continues to be a popular fair attraction offering milking demonstrations and an ice cream dairy bar. (Photograph by Stephen Mease.)

When the COVID-19 pandemic forced high schools to cancel traditional graduations, the exposition offered its facilities to host a drive-in ceremony. Here, Champlain Valley High School teachers and staff welcome graduates to the celebration. (Photograph by Stephen Mease.)

After it outgrew its tented graduation ceremonies in Burlington, Champlain College relocated its pomp and circumstance to the exposition in 2019. The ease of parking, as well as the size and comfort of the indoor accommodations in the Robert E. Miller Expo Centre, made it a popular change. (Photograph by Stephen Mease.)

Essex Junction High School held its 2020 graduation outdoors at the exposition during the pandemic. Seniors and others wore masks to receive diplomas, while family and friends watched from their cars drive-in theater style. (Photograph courtesy the Essex Reporter.)

The pandemic summer of 2020 had some bright sides when South Burlington concert promoter Higher Ground set up the stage and big screen at the exposition for its summer and fall concert series. As a result, several area high schools were able to piggyback use of the facilities for their outdoor drive-in-style graduations.

The fairgrounds easily accommodated the long lines of cars coming to pick up food boxes from the Farm to Family food donation program during the pandemic in 2020.

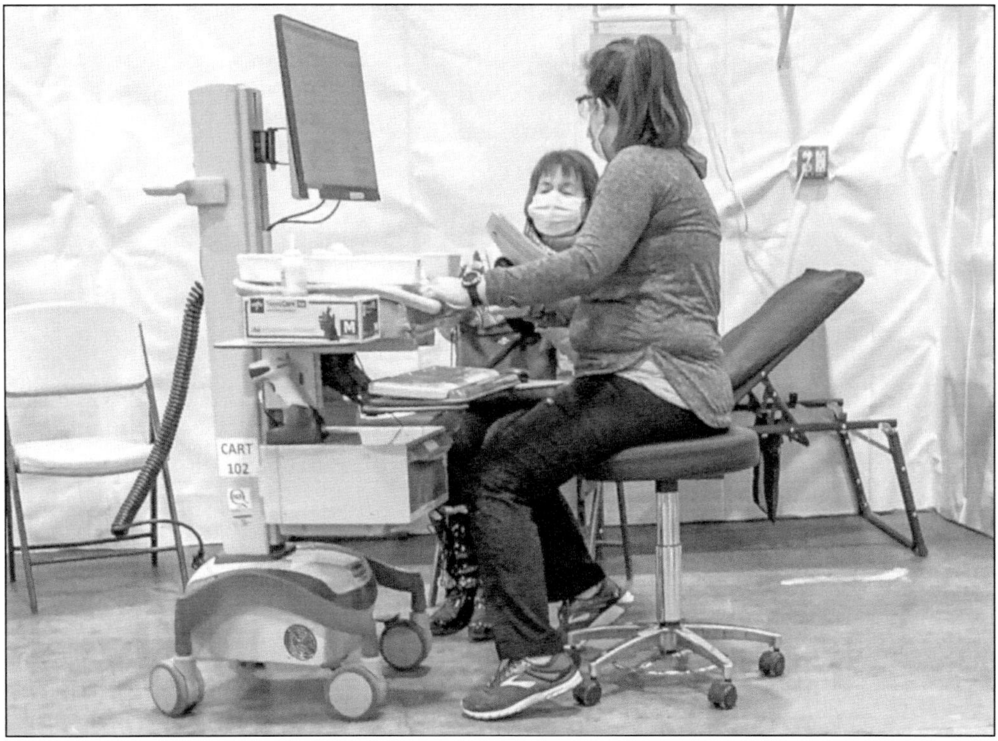

When regular events were canceled due to the pandemic, the exposition became an emergency medical center assembled by the Vermont National Guard in Expo North and South. It also served as a University of Vermont Medical Center COVID-19 testing site, and in early 2021, the exposition was one of Vermont's largest mass vaccination sites.

With careful planning and an eye to safety, the 2021 Champlain Valley Fair was once again "The 10 Best Days of Summer," with a full lineup of agriculture, free entertainment, concerts, carnival, and rides.

A new Champlain Valley Exposition history exhibit made its debut in 2021, researched and designed by Stephen Mease, this book's author. It replaced a display developed in 1996 for the exposition's 75th anniversary. (Photograph by Cheryl Dorschner.)